Our Kind of
Polygamy

David G. Maillu

HEINEMANN KENYA

NAIROBI

Published by
Heinemann Kenya Ltd.,
Kijabe Street,
P.O. Box 45314,
NAIROBI

First published 1988

ISBN 9966—46—381—X

Typeset by Middlepak Typesetters,
P.O. Box 60975,
NAIROBI

Printed by
General Printers Ltd.,
P.O. Box 18001
NAIROBI

Contents

CHAPTER EIGHT

CHAPTER NINE

CHAPTER TEN

CHAPTER ELEVEN

Introduction

Let me start off by saying that, in spite of the influence of the extensive amount of book research that I had to consider in the shaping of the central opinion of this book, after listening to all the debates on the subject and, sometimes, getting involved in the debates, what I say in this book should be seen or construed as a personal reflection on this controversial subject.

This book was inspired by a number of things. One of them being the kind of press debates that have been going on about the merits and demerits, if not the sense and nonsense, of polygamy as articulated by modern men and women, policy makers, moralists, a specific group of Christians, and the dialectics of the traditional and modern Africa coloured by the western cultural interpretations and influences. Secondly, by the kind of questions that modern young Africans are raising on the subject in search of an answer, obviously, to the problems they themselves and their individual families and friends face in the decision to be or not to be polygamist. Maybe the least inspiration to write the book came from the questions I was constantly asked by Westerners, Whites in particular, in many countries of the world, regarding the philosophy, or sense, if any, of the African polygamy. I was also inspired by the response I got from the numerous lectures that I delivered on the subject to peoples of all walks of life.

The most persistent and burning question today regarding Polygamy is whether it is a civilised practice, or uncivilised, if not primitive and irrelevant in modern Africa.

I am not going to prove whether or not polygamy exists in Africa. Neither am I out to sell the cow of polygamy to those who have no sympathy for it. My concern here is simply to look at the issue from the standpoint of contributing to the ongoing debate and, if possible, or as far as possible, offer my own interpretations, conclusions, and advice where I feel there is a need for such.

It is also my contention that, since polygamy has been outside the educational curriculum and the western cultural ethos that are influencing Africa have been treating it as undesirable, if not a taboo, the aesthetics of polygamy are increasingly getting forgotten and, altogether, the practice has been exposed to many misunderstandings. All that, in turn, is creating many social problems that could, otherwise, be minimised by giving the phenomenon the study and attention it requires.

I cannot write a book of this kind, or rather tackle this subject without taking a definite stand. What I am saying in the book, therefore, is what I believe in: hence my personal opinion and commitment. I make this commitment on behalf of those to whom my kind of argument carries weight and who endeavour to solve a social problem. I also believe that somebody somewhere should be able to stand up and give an answer, even if a lame one, to the serious questions of polygamy that are being raised today.

Polygamy is an issue that involves a man and a woman. These are the two who make it. Unfortunately, it is one subject in which you can only write or speak about either as a man or as a woman. The quick questions that you are asked if you are a man who happens to have written a book of this kind are: Why do you feel so confident about making commitments of this nature for and on behalf of women? Is this surely what you would say if you were a woman? Or, would a woman reflect on the assertions or rules or whatever, which you are advancing here?

A quick answer to these questions is that I am a man writer, looking at an issue that affects men's life, and, first and foremost, I can only see and say what I have said in this book from the point of view of a man. Otherwise, if I were a woman I would write it only from the point of a woman. This is, and should be a free dialogue therefore, in which either man or woman has room to say his or her bit. For that reason, I make no apology should I, in some parts of this book, miss to represent woman to the very last detail after all the efforts I have made to represent her views fully. Where I have failed to attain the finesse of a woman, it was not my wish to do so, but my failure and weakness as a man (naturally) to feel things like a woman.

Let me be brief by saying that this is a man's view on the subject, and I advance the challenge that it would be a big contribution also, at another time, to hear a woman's view on the subject. Perhaps then we can compare notes and settle to a synthesis of the two.

Finally, even though polygamy is a universal subject that deserves to be treated as such in any discussion, should the views expressed herein sound too foreign in some parts to non-African readers, it is because I wrote it (I had no other choice) purely as an African, coloured by the

African perceptions and experiences. I do not, therefore, pretend to produce a universal manual for solving polygamy problems. Mine is rather a case study of polygamy with African sensitivity as the base, qualified by the values of the Kenyan homestead, as whence the smoke comes, therein the fire is.

A book on polygamy is, no doubt, bound to touch on some of the most emotional and delicate parts of the community and, let me admit it, I do not regard myself clever enough to get away with everything without, in one way or other, making some kind of assumptions even unconsciously. In that case, I accept the liability and apologize for them.

David G. Maillu

CHAPTER ONE

AFRICAN POLYGAMY

Our kind of polygamy

What is polygamy?
A definition of polygamy is a must before any discussion can be made.

A polygamist is simply a man who is married to more than one wife, living with them at the same time. Polygamy, therefore, is the act of being a polygamist.

Polygamy, or plural marriage as it is called sometimes, is found throughout the world in a variety of forms that are determined by the culture of the people. Among the western peoples, the familiar term is consecutive polygamy. That is, marrying and living with one wife at a time, and this amounts to no more than a serial monogamy in which one husband is engaged consecutively in descreet monogamous unions.

Africa has practised polygamy as far back as the records can take us. In other words, polygamy is and has always been a way of life in Africa. There is a great belief in Europe and America, for example, that any native of Africa is a polygamist. Or at least, he is a potential polygamist. Most Whitemen see polygamy as an attribute of primitiveness, and they think that the African cannot really attain civilization unless he has discontinued polygamy and adopted monogamy.

Since the arrival of the Whiteman in Africa, with the joint effort of the church, he has been doing his best to abolish polygamy. Indeed, a great deal has been done to wipe out polygamy in colonial Africa. Yet the tradition has continued to survive. The colonial church in particular, has been fighting against the tradition on the basis that it is incompatible with the Bible; whereas the colonial administration went against it with the claim that it is not in keeping with modern civilisation.

But is polygamy really a primitive practice? Is it really unchristian? Has it a positive and moral part to play in our lives? What is the cause of polygamy?

Before proceeding to articulate the central thought upon which our kind of polygamy rests, it is good to first and foremost establish the bare fact that, in spite of the noise that is made with regard to the pervasiveness of polygamy in Africa, polygamy is usually practised by only a small percentage of the population of any given country. Why is that so? Simply because there is only a small surplus of women who are available to married men as second, third, fourth or whatever number of wives. Nature does not produce as many women as would make it possible for every man or nearly every man in Africa to be a polygamist.

The population census of Kenya of 1979 gives the sex ratio of 51% female and 49% male. I am told that the same ratio holds for a good number of African countries that include Zambia, Zimbabwe, and Uganda. So, there is only about 2% surplus of women who are potentially available for polygamous relations.

Let us take the population of Africa to be 600,000,000 people. Hypothetically speaking, 51% of that figure is female and the rest is male; hence:

Females — 306,000,000
Males — 294,000,000
Surplus — 12,000,000

What is obvious from this number is that, of the 294 million potential polygamist males, only a few would get a second wife if each man were restricted to only one more wife. This is because, theoretically, the surplus is only 12 million against the big demand. In practice, the proportion of polygamists is even smaller because some have more than two wives. Usually, those are the rich chiefs, kings, and nobles.

However, sticking to the hypothetical number of two wives per polygamist, then the number of polygamists would be no more than the number of women. In other words there would be 12 million polygamists in a population of 294 million men in Africa. 282 million married men would then be monogamist.

If Africa operates according to the same biological laws as other countries of the world, it is more or less correct to conclude that the ratio of the surplus in question is the same everywhere in the world.

Traditional Africa has always been taking care of the surplus women in the society by giving them homes and husbands. What has the western system been doing with its surplus? I shall try to explain later.

Talking about polygamy, the question you get from non-sympathizers is: Why should a man be allowed to marry two or three wives when a woman is not allowed to marry two or three husbands? That is a sensible question, but then, according to the above statistics, men being fewer than women, it would be difficult for a married woman to find another man to marry as a second husband, since all men, as it were, are already in the hands of other women. Perhaps if the number of men was larger than that of women, such a thing would not be unheard of. Then there is the other question opposing polygamy: Is it possible to love two women equally? This is the kind of question which implies that a man who marries a second wife while he lives with the first one, will naturally be forced to love one wife less than the other. I shall examine the meaning of love elsewhere in this book in order to answer this question.

Traditionally, there are a number of reasons that drive the African into polygamy, or rather, that urge the single girl or woman to enter into a marriage contract with a man who already has another wife. It would be appropriate here to proceed to examine the very major ones.

Childlessness and adoption

In Africa, a child is not merely a child but a great event. Childlessness is not merely an unfavourable incident, but a calamity. And, as one anthropologist puts it, to an African, marriage is not an event, but a process that, if normal and blessed, culminates in the birth of a child.

The first natural acceptance to the African, in so far as woman-to-man sexual relation in marriage is concerned, is that their coming together is primarily to procreate. This is seen as a divine call. He knows that life can continue on earth only when the old give way to the birth of the young, and that the tree that does not bear brings an end to its own kind. That the old make the bridge to the future by bearing young ones. And a recognition that life appears to have only two major shifts: one in which the old nurse the young because the young are too young and helpless; the second shift when the young have to nurse the old because the old are too weak to help themselves. That is, the two generations are purely complementary. Or metaphorically speaking, the two ages are the two hands of the same person so that what the right hand has taken is passed over to the left hand, and in any performance, the two hands desperately need each other.

Traditional thought sees the child, therefore, as the second hand of the parent. To have no child would then be equivalent to having only one hand. If it is by God's design that one does not have a child, that is understood and sympathized with; however, if it be by personal choice to be childless, then such is seen as a grave misunderstanding of the basic requirements of life; hence, cruelty not only to one's own life but to that of the people who have to live with the childless. Such denial is also seen as a violation of the law of creation.

Each life is understood as a link of the eternal chain of existence that stretches from the unknown past into the unkown future. It is by divine law that man should not break this chain by a deliberate refusal to have children. He should see and understand himself as not purely his own being, but a link between the living and the dead. In the event of his death, he will live through his own blood and spirit that he leaves behind in a child of his own. Then, as long as that child relays forward the life of the parent by a turn of having his own children, his grandparents as well as all those who came before those grandparents shall never perish, but will live forever.

If that torch of life given by God is allowed to extinguish, God or nature or whatever force is behind creation, has a way of punishing those who do not pass it over to the next through procreation. It is an olympic torch that was started by the force and wish of creation commonly referred to as God, back in the unknown beginning and it must be borne forward into eternity.

In practice, you know that for sure, sooner or later, your energy will yield to old age. Distances which were short during your youth become long ones in old age, and it is at that time when you will need the energy of someone else to enable you reach the destination. In your old age, you will need food, shelter and, above all, human company and love. How can you then afford to leave these things to chance, hoping that at that desperate age a good Samaritan would come to your aid? The best you can do therefore to assure self-protection is to have a child of your own. For in life, there are certain misfortunes that can be averted by no one else but your own child. As the saying goes, blood is thicker than water. If you

4

choose not to have a child of your own, do not weep over such misfortunes and do not expect sympathy from others; as another proverb goes: let there be no weeping for those who die by their own choice through suicide.

Whether or not the child keeps to the parental hope that inspired his birth, what is obvious is that a person who has had children lives a life that is more realised and more rewarding and richer in terms of human experiences than one who chose to have no children.

Having children has been seen and understood as a kind of natural insurance policy against the unseen bad circumstances which might rob a person of his loved one, of his shelter, food and company. It is a move to ensure that when you weep, there will be, or there is likely to be, someone who matters to see your tears. Yet a child is much more than that. As the Luo community of Kenya puts it, to have a child is to have a mirror for looking at your back. Over and above, your child is a reflection of yourself in whom you see, study, understand and realise yourself. Your child is a parable of your own life; a parable that tells you, 'Look here, this is you and these are your works.' Having a child makes you take leave out of yourself in order to have an outside view of yourself which should be, by itself, an exciting experience.

Through your own child, it becomes possible for you, in a way, to live and be what otherwise is difficult or impossible to live in your own experience. How often have you heard a parent declare, 'As I failed to achieve such and such, I will try my best to make it possible for my child to achieve it.'? In other words, the achievement will be made on behalf of the parent; hence, it will be a success to both parties.

There was a quarrel between a boy and a man in which the adult had slapped the boy in anger. After crying, the boy warned the man, 'Just wait, one day I will be big and strong enough to fight you.' But the man retorted, 'That time will never come. By the time you will be big and strong enough to fight me or beat me up, I will have big and strong children to fight for me.'

The philosophy of that man was: "I am what I am and, if a later misfortune renders me what I am not now, my children shall reform and redeem me.'

The child is the crown of the marriage. He is the fulfilment of the promise of love and survival. He is seen as a blessing of God, and the greenlight that you are now allowed to proceed to your destination.

The fear of getting old without a child is comparable to the fear of going to war without weapons. The fear of falling sick without a child, the fear of dying without a child, the fear of extinction—such fears are, indeed, crippling and traumatic experiences to many people.

The birth of the child has another psychological meaning or value to the parent. His birth is the first stamp of fulfilment of the requirements and expectations of maturity. It says, 'Here, you are now a full human being; nothing whatsoever is wrong with you, so relax;' After this, you do not suffer from any psychological feeling that you are or could be a deviant to social norms as happens to many women and men who never have a child of their own.

There is the economic factor tied to the birth of children in a given family. In a situation where the economic structure is based on the labour force of the family (which is commonplace in traditional African families) the continuation of birth of children in that family has, indeed, substantial economic implications. The majority of Africans in such situations grow poorer as they grow older for the obvious reason that they cannot produce as much, as energetically and effectively, as they could when they were young. New births to the family every now and then is the replacement of the economic cells that have been or are wearing out.

It is against the above background that one should view and understand the problems of a person—man and woman—whose efforts to get a child have been frustrated. Every effort is made to get that child if the wife is unable to bear one. To the husband, the question of resorting to another woman becomes a reality. This is the first urge to become a polygamist. And for the survival of the spirit of her own marriage together with the economic security of her old age, the childless wife is forced by her own necessity to consider a co-wife as the redeemer.

In traditional Africa, daughters are brought up for marriage, or at least, bearing the faith that they will eventually get married in order to start a 'saving account' for their own lives too, besides fulfilling the natural urge to have a male partner. They therefore grow up with the knowledge that one day they will leave the parents' home to start their own home since, in nearly all cases, it is the girl who goes to the man's home to start a marriage. Sons are, therefore, brought up to live with or within the domain of the parents and, for this reason, they and their wives become the custodians of the parents' security and social life.

Nearly everywhere in Africa, it is an embarrassment or a taboo for a parent, regardless of his or her needs, to go and live with his or her married daughter in order to secure social protection. It is equally embarrassing for the married daughter to bring her husband along to her parents' home in order to take care of her ailing or needy parents; neither is it feasible for her to come alone to live with them as to attend to their needs.

This is why a couple gets restless when they get a series of daughters without a single son. Although the degree of disappointment may differ from the husband to the wife, what they have in common is to begin to see a future in which they will be left alone in a home with no one else to relate to for their own protection. They start to see a life where they will have no one around them to love them. Of course, they are aware that something may still happen, in that one of their daughters may have an unhappy marriage or be driven into a situation that brings her back home permanently or that, perhaps, one of the successful daughters may try to provide for their needs. However, all this becomes at best, excellent material for guesswork. They would be taking too much of a chance to build any hopes on such speculative grounds. That is the kind of chance that could be taken only when all other alternatives have been exhausted.

A second marriage may give the family this most desired son. Over and above, and for emotional reasons too—this happens all over the world—having a son is always more cherished than having a daughter. If couples were given a choice to have only one child and had to choose the sex, the majority would chose a son. Many cases have been reported in some eastern countries outside Africa where the life of the child is terminated medically or neglected when it is a daughter. Some of those countries have reduced the number of females in the community drastically enough to tamper with the natural balance—creating a society in which there are more men than women.

Where the family has been getting a series of daughters, the father may feel justified in trying his luck through a second wife. This may be with or without the approval of the first wife. It would be to her disadvantage if she resists the move for one reason or other—there are always many reasons to make her oppose the move. The second wife may be a girl or a widow or a divorcee (and it would be to the widow's advantage if she brings a living son to the family). The second wife with children is possible only in communities where the divorcee or widow is allowed to transfer her children to the second marriage. In many cases she is not allowed to take the children with her from the home of her first marriage. That means she goes to the second marriage alone.

In most cases however, the second wife is a girl. There have been many situations in which the first wife has had a hand in proposing the second marriage and even going to the extent of initiating the engagement based on her personal choice of the bride. The fact that the sex of the child is determined by the sperm of the father, is a secret that has remained hidden to men until recently when medical science came up with the proof. Hence, even when the wife produced a series of daughters, the husband felt justified in laying the blame squarely on the wife, instead of on himself, for failing to get a son. However, the issue is far more complex than what can be said here in that a man may fail to produce a son with one woman but produce one with another woman because of what may be called blood compatibility and incompatibility.

African civilization considers it both inhuman and a mark of immaturity to victimise the first wife by way of divorce simply because she has failed to have a child or deliver a child of the desired sex. Polygamy is, no doubt, the kindest solution in the case of a wife who is infertile. It is much better for her to remain the wife of that man instead of being thrown out to suffer the impossible task of looking for another husband.

The question remains—what if the husband is the infertile one? Is the wife allowed to marry a second man?

Without medical science, it was difficult to determine whether or not it was the husband who was infertile, much more so if such a husband was still capable of having sexual relations. However, different communities have always had a way of checking this. If there was proof of the husband's infertility therefore, the most commonly used method of getting a child or children, was to secretly appoint the husband's cousin from the maternal or paternal side or even a brother to fulfil the duty. But in every case, the choice had to be a man of integrity who had the moral capacity to guard the image of the legal husband and that of his home as a whole. Again, different communities have had different ways and rituals of officiating this move. Moreover, the man chosen has to be acceptable to the wife. This creates a situation in which, the wife has, as it were, two husbands. But strictly speaking, the second man remains always at the level of the concubine. All the children born to this family carry the name of the legal husband even though biologically they are the off-springs of the second man.

The desire to have the child may be caused by the anxiety as to who should inherit the father's property (or the mother's, in some African communities) after the death of the parents. Or who should take over some family responsibilities that usually fall upon the father's home in the event of a crisis.

In an African set up, what we strictly know today as child adoption is extremely rare, since a child has been so important to marriage that parents would very seldom give it up for adoption. As a result the number of children available for adoption has been very small. Instead, the kind of adoption that has been widely practised in Africa has been achieved through marriage of the mother of the child, doubtlessly, a practice that is superior to the modern adoption method, and one which has excellent moral values. A child grows up as an emotionally and psychologically mature person if and when brought up or is attached to, at least, one of his or her natural parents and within a marital and legal institution. Marriage contracted mainly because of securing a child is thus seen, more or less, as a form of child adoption. Isn't it a noble idea, too, to adopt the helpless mother of the helpless child?

Sexual Incompatibility and Inequality

It is common knowledge that different people have different sexual capacities. It is not always possible to match couples sexually. Whereas there may be a man who is satisfied completely by having sexual relations once a week, another may find it really hard-going if he does not have it every other day and perhaps twice on a particular occasion. Some men can easily accommodate having intercourse fifteen times a week (of course in rather extreme cases). But there are others who may comfortably have it once a fortnight or so. Nature is simply erratic.

There is an obvious problem when the husband is highly sexed against a wife who is not. His high demand can very easily be a great strain to her, worse so if her health is not excellent or when she is pregnant, or under particular psychological difficulties.

It is an over-simplification of the issue to think that any amount of psychiatric or religious treatment would solve the problem. The natural way of solving it, is through the natural outlet. If such a highly sexed husband does not get his satisfaction from the wife, he is likely to obtain it from outside by all means. African psychiatric advice to the man with excessive sexual potence is to marry a second wife and stop torturing his wife. The Akamba people of Kenya have a saying that if you want to tie a 'wild' man down, marry him to many wives. To divorce his wife on the basis of her sexual shortcomings is an act of immaturity. For one thing, such a divorce does not guarantee that the second marriage would be any better.

It is also immature and sheer selfishness for the wife who knows that she is not capable of satisfying her husband sexually, to pretend that she can handle the situation while actually forcing him to suppress his desire. This may have some very unpleasant consequences. Instead, she should allow him (sometimes with bitterness of course) to solve the problem by marrying a second wife.

In other situations, it may happen that, the sexually under-charged wife improves with time. Any move that gives her a natural allowance for the development of her sexual response is something that should be highly appreciated. The fact that the two are sexually unequal should not be allowed to terminate a marriage that, otherwise, may have other good things to share. Even in some healthy relationships between wives and husbands, sexual differences do exist. If such incompatibilities can be solved by other gentler ways and retain the solidarity of the marriage, that is commendable.

When the above question appears to smack of male chauvinism, there is the other question asked, 'What if, on the contrary, the wife is oversexed against a husband who is lowsexed—is she allowed or should she, take another husband?'

What we often forget easily concerning the union between man and woman is that it is a mutual agreement and not a regimentation. It is a joint venture of the two, with some amount of inbuilt allowances to help each other solve their individual poblems, be they sexual, economic, or whatever. The question of whether the wife is 'allowed' or permitted to get another husband implies regimentation or strict laid down regulations to run the marriage. When the two are getting married, they are aware, without any verbal expression, of their possible limitations. Their success in the marriage depends very much on the degree of flexibility of each to let the other live with minimum strain, and not on the vows and observance of any marriage laws.

It is not unheard of in the African community for a woman to have extra-marital love relations. Women who have higher sexual demands than can be adequately quenched by the husband have always had their own ways of satisfying that need. But it is good to start off by appreciating that man's sexual requirements are far more forceful than woman's whose needs are, by biological reasons, less pronounced. For example, her sexual requirements are affected significantly by:

(a) pregnancy, particularly at the earliest and later stages of that pregnancy.
(b) childbirth, and for quite some time after that it becomes impossible for her to engage in sexual relations.
(c) menstruation
(d) hormonal changes during menopause.

Man's sexual urge does not suffer from any such periods. It is continuous; so it is not surprising that the frequency of his sexual needs is much higher than that of woman. It is this frequency which, if naturally accentuated, may easily propel him to seek sexual release from a second partner much faster than the woman's frequency would drive her to a second man.

Of course, it is equally selfish and immature for a husband who knows that his wife's sexual needs surpass his to simply silence her by the use of external force. Yet, this is not the kind of thing in which he can tell her, 'Beatrice, you can solve the problem by having a boyfriend behind the scene.' Her involvement with another man is bound to have more devastating consequences than her husband's affair with another woman. It is the kind of thing which is likely to interfere heavily with her own image of personal integrity. Her own children, for example, would react more unfavourably when they find out that their mother has a lover, than if they discover that their father is having an affair with another woman. They would rather hear that their father stole something than to hear that their mother played the thief. It appears that her role has been naturally and culturally slanted or cultivated to be the kingpost of her home's morals. It is this expectation, in addition to the nature of her sexual requirements, which prevents her from asking for two husbands or more. One of the questions asked in connection with this is whether she can really contain or handle two husbands for, in this case, the issue at hand is one of contentment and not merely the acquisition of another husband.

Even when a woman is in a position to enjoy in extra-marital relations without endangering her marriage, she appears to be contented with far less than what would satisfy a man. The old saying that man is a polygamous creature has not been done away with by any amount of education and modernisation. In other words, man is sexually greedier than woman. In most instances, a woman is contented with one husband so long as he is loving and gives her most of the attention she needs. What a man may do with his sexual surplus is different from what a woman would do with hers. It appears to be so much so because of self-image, taste, biological differences and, of course, cultural reasons.

Children born and bred in a cultural set up where polygamy is accepted, grow up with liberal ideas about polygamous relationships. A married man in the western world who has a lover can expect some degree of tolerance from his community. This is because that approach to life has been culturally developed.

A man who has ten wives knows only too well that he cannot sexually provide for them satisfactorily. He then exercises a high degree of tolerance if not acceptance, of his wives' sexual engagements with other men which, in this case, cannot be described as acts of infidelity. In this context, the word 'fidelity' becomes more of a western concept. For a better understanding, we shall discuss in detail elsewhere the sexual differences of man and woman.

Inheriting Widows (Levirate)

The nobility and integrity of the homestead depends on how ready its owners are to take up responsibilities as and when crises arise. The best that can be given to a woman who has lost her husband through death, is either a replacement or a helper. This, in the context of our civilisation, is regarded as positive not only to her physical and psychological requirements but also to the well-being of her children.

This is the only home that the children have known. Their friends and relatives are here. Where else in the world could serve them better than here? To make it possible for the children and their mother to continue living here where their true home is, the mother of the children should find favour in a male member of her husband's family. If there is a brother whom she likes and he is married, arrangements are made for him to take her into his care as an additional wife. The wife of that brother is supposed to understand and sympathize with the situation. Alternatively, the husband's cousin or brother-in-law may take over the widow. However, the qualification attached to this practice is that such a 'caretaker' must be a man of upright standing. It is also not by force that she should take a man she does not like.

To leave the widow with her children out in the cold is seen as a great lack of love for the family. The best tribute that can be paid to the dead man is to take care of his family. Also, it is only natural that she should be practically sympathized with.

I am not trying to create the impression that all continues to be fantastic after the death of the husband. The takeover may create friction with the wife of the caretaker; but even his wife is aware (she too has been culturally moulded into this awareness) that tomorrow it may be her turn. Whatever service or allowances she extends to the widow therefore, is eventually a contribution to her own security in this home as well as a promotion of the integrity of this homestead.

In America and western European countries, and it seems among the so-called modernised Africans, the death of a husband throws his wife out into the cold and insecurity. She becomes a creature to be pitied and avoided, particularly if she has a large family. She is feared, distrusted and hated by married women who think she poses a threat to their marriage. She and her children become lonely and exposed to all kinds of psychological problems. In traditional Africa, loneliness of widows and of children who have lost their father is virtually unknown.

Labour Force

Shift farming has encouraged polygamy too. Due to the establishment of new areas of farming and cattle grazing, the small family suffers a split. It is not always easy to move the family around with the changing conditions of weather. Where the husband is forced to stay away from home in the new area of farming, and where the situation is a temporary one, he deems it unwise to disrupt the established order of the home.

In such a case, both the husband and wife try to strike a compromise in the nature of a second wife. The first wife would maintain this side of the family while the second wife maintains the other side. The decision is even more convenient where the shifting keeps recurring from time to time.

Employing people to help in this task has not been practical, because in the first place traditional Africa has not been operating on a money-economy. Secondly, great emphasis has been placed on self reliance and freedom of the individual, even though, in some quarters, some form of employment has been practised, the society has always been aware that an employee comes with other constraints.

The backbone of the traditional economy has been the trust of the members of the family in terms of what they can produce and save for their own survival. So where the mode of production has required a large labour force, there has not been a better alternative than the expansion of that family by establishing polygamous relations. This is because the coming of a woman to a home brings other family hands in the form of children. The children of a plural marriage have great importance in the economics of the family: the more they are, the healthier the economy is. The hands of the first wife are not enough for a prosperous and secure living.

In this case, low birth rate is not an asset but a liability. A man whose wife has produced only one or two children, obviously considers increasing the number of his family hands by bringing another wife into the family. Also given the high rate of child mortality in traditional Africa, the desire to increase the security of the family through producing more children becomes quite understandable.

However, in modern times and as the society moves from communal economy to the individualized, industrial and money-economy, it is obvious that family-based labour force shall lose its significance. But the new economy is bound to create other constraints, conditions or modifications, which would justify the continuation of polygamy.

The African family is an extended one. When a husband takes up a job in the city, for example, it is not always possible for him to bring the entire family to live in the city. For one thing, his pay may not be sufficient to afford his family's accommodation; this becomes even more difficult if the family in question is a big one, or where the man also has to care for his ageing parents and other relatives. It is common knowledge that most of the urban workers in the lower income group do not, and cannot afford to live with their families in their places of work. Such family splits are also made necessary by the need for the wives to engage in farm work in the village to subsidize the high cost of living for the family. '

In the new urban-rural placement of the family, the arrangement that is usually made is for the wife of the urban worker to pay her husband a visit now and then in the city. The husband reciprocates by travelling to the countryside as and when the pocket allows. This movement and separation creates many problems especially considering that some people have to travel long distances to work in the city. The old situation in which the farmer found himself away from home, lonely and without a helper has now been duplicated. The husband who moves with his family to the place of work is comparable to the nomad who is forced to follow the good weather for his survival.

The city worker who is thus separated from his wife and family, whose salary is not enough to afford the trips to and from the country home, is forced, (if he cannot really exercise any self-control), to look for a complementary helper. If he is an honest man, he opts for a second wife, frequently, a woman who works in town who can alternate with his first wife in giving him the company he desires.

He cannot simply go ahead and divorce his first wife because the second marriage was not brought about by any fault in the first marriage. But it would be good for the husband to appreciate the fact that by contracting another marriage, he has thrown himself into bigger economic problems, because the second wife comes with her own economic and emotional demands.

To avoid this economic 'disaster' as it has come to be known, some of the urban men have been practising what they call the 'hit-and-run' or 'one-night' marriage, a situation in the urban centres. For, when his pocket cannot afford a second wife, or if he fears that his first wife is likely to reject the idea of a co-wife, the only solution at his disposal is to go to a concubine or a prostitute. He would opt for a mistress if he is in a more favourable economic situation. If not, he would maintain some loose friendship with single or married women for his emotional and sexual needs. This appears to be the same old wine put in new containers—an economic dictation.

It is over-simplification to try to offer any moral advice on this urban-rural problem, if one has to see it as a problem, simply because the issues involved are so basic. Men and women are very much aware of the physical and spiritual dangers of prostitution just as drunkards are aware of the hazards of taking too much alcohol, but such awareness does not stop them from the practice. In other words, people do not make mistakes so much out of ignorance, but out of ignoring what they know or are aware of. Anything else can be said but, morally, it is much better to engage in honest polygamy than in prostitution and concubinage.

Moral Obligation

Traditional Africa dispised the hit-and-run game in which a man makes a girl pregnant and runs away from any responsibility brought about by that pregnancy. When a man made a girl pregnant, he was expected to bear the responsibility of the safety and care of both the mother and the child. Knowing the problems of a girl who had become a mother, the only way to sympathize with her was to marry her, unless she did not want to marry him or there were other major constraints.

This move did not only maintain the dignity of the girl, but that of the man too. Marrying the mother of his child created a good atmosphere for the child to grow up in a world in which he was accepted but not abused. Naturally, the fear of taking up such responsibility kept many married men from getting involved with girls and, hence, offered excellent moral checkpoints.

Another quick question raised in connection with this is: 'Why should a married man make a girl pregnant, let alone getting involved with her?'

One answer is that it simply happens in spite of the ugliness of the action. Another reason is that man does not live in a perfect world. Due to one reason or other (this should not justify the action) some married men have always got involved with girls and created such a liability. The fault may be in the man himself or in the girl, or both. The action can also be influenced by an external or internal force, physical or even spiritual, social or economic.

Because of the economic implications, most men who find themselves in such situations today, do their very best to evade the responsibility even if it means blackmailing the girl or using threats against her life. But the man of integrity, like the noble traditional man, will always take the moral path by bearing the responsibility.

Other Marital Shortcomings

Any living thing is capable of falling sick or developing an abnormality. It is possible for a man to enjoy a healthy marriage with a woman for some time during which things run smoothly. But then other problems begin to arise. Their cause may be external or internal. Maybe in the long run his wife begins to take him for granted; or she eventually becomes less responsible or lazy, or she acquires some bad characteristics that do not please him today; or she finally becomes disillusioned about the marriage or the composition of his family and does not any more compromise with the family.

Instead of taking drastic and rather inhuman divorce measures against such a wife, traditionally the husband considers marrying a second wife. This move tends to give the first wife a chance to correct herself; that is, if she is the one who is in the wrong. Of course, the fault may lie with the husband too. But the issue here is one in which the husband does not find any favour with his wife and he is forced by his own will to seek the company of another woman.

The second marriage, too, saves the first wife from the embarrassment and public ridicule that sometimes accompany divorce. The children are also spared the problems that are brought about by a broken home. . . Even when people have fallen out of love with each other, they still may have other things they appreciate of each other. Polygamy makes it possible for the couple to continue to enjoy those other aspects of the first marriage that are pleasant. The first wife may be a witch, but a witch who has other excellent qualities. The husband may be an impossible fanatic or idealist, but he may be a good father to his children, or the economic pillar of the first marriage.

When a wife is faced with a divorce threat, she cannot maintain steady thoughts with which to reflect on issues and take appreciable action.

17

Polygamy gives her the patience and the time she needs to correct herself or tame the man if he is wild. Perhaps his complaint is an exaggeration of some minor faults in the wife; perhaps he is a man who expects too much from his wife. He may be the kind of man who does not know himself, but one who thinks or feels that he is misunderstood by his wife and, for that reason, he decides to marry a woman who really understands him.

So, he goes ahead and marries his dream, perhaps only to be jostled from his sleep by reality to discover that he did not solve the problem because he, himself, had been the problem right from the beginning. From now on, he begins to see his wife in a better perspective and his admiration for her, which he had lost, begins to rekindle.

Only polygamy could have given him such excellent opportunity to learn and understand himself without having to go through the ordeal of divorce. And now that he has discovered himself, he can be a better husband.

Traditional African marital custom has excellent shockabsorbers for human shortcomings. The custom is generous to the wife, child, husband, relatives, widow, single girl, the sick and the unfortunate, the friend and the neighbour. One wonders whether it could be any better.

We are urged today to take marital problems to a marriage counsellor, psychologist, or a psychiatrist. While this advice or approach is sound in the treatment of ailing marriages, it is so easy to forget that only a very small number of our married population can afford to see a marriage counsellor who may not even have received any training in the treatment of problems connected with polygamy and extended family relations. Traditional Africa did the least in institutionalizing and commercializing knowledge; whatever she got, she disseminated into the day-to-day lives of people and hardly anyone paid anybody for being counselled.

Wife's bad health

Traditional Africa has not been advanced in medicine. There have been so many cases of prolonged illnesses, lameness acquired later in life and many other physical and psychological problems. Even in countries where health care is advanced, invalidity is not unknown. In all such cases the husband would be encouraged to think of a second marriage, first and foremost, to give the first wife time to recover. Moreover, the new co-wife would help nursing the sick one besides giving motherly support to the children of the first marriage. She would also take over other duties of the first wife, and look after some of her interests.

If the invalidity is sexual, a second marriage would obviously be the cure. Traditional Africa did not encourage secret, extra-marital relations outside the home. Such relations were a disgrace not only to the husband, but the children and the image of the homestead.

It would be completely misleading to think that, because health care has been modernized, our societies have got over the problem of invalidity. Generally, it is still only the people who are economically very strong who can apply the magic or money to rid their family of invalidity. The problem stays for many people. In which case, the prospects of a second wife joining a family because of the bad health of the first wife is bound to continue, especially so when we consider the fact that the idea of divorcing the first wife on health grounds continues to be both ridiculous and inhuman in the minds of the men and families affected.

CHAPTER TWO

Love and Polygamy

Americans and western Europeans wonder how a man can be married to two or more wives at the same time and, in some instances, in the same space and yet love them effectively. The question asked is the one we posed earlier on, regarding how a man can share his love equally between two or more wives. Some think that only brutality and dictatorship can keep the wives silent because there is not enough love to keep them smiling.

At this juncture, it is important that we examine what love is and how it has been, and could be expressed in polygamy. What is this most talked and sung about word, LOVE? A dictionary definition describes it as *a warm, kind feeling, or fondness or affection and tender devotion*. One example is a parent's love for her or his child.

When used to describe general things, love means, *a great liking for*; hence, love of music, adventure, travelling, games, money, God, and so on. But it is the love between man and woman that is called into a discussion here. When a man tells a woman, 'I love you', what actually does he mean? When a woman tells a man, 'I love you,' what does she mean? Can that statement have only one meaning?

'I love you', said by a man or woman to the other, may simply be an expression of admiration that does not go deep. Or it may be an expression of sexual attraction which is not guaranteed to last because it may also be a situational feeling said either under great sexual tension or some kind of temporary emotional frustration. We have witnessed so many such 'loves' coming and getting consummated today and disappearing tomorrow. Christians may call such love 'lust'.

Love, in this case can, therefore, be situational.

The other obvious meaning of 'I love you', if said heartily by a man to a woman with no blood relationship, means or implies that she is good enough to be his wife. However, this 'good enough' may be (and usually it is) based on a number of valued characteristics of the woman. When those qualities are valued and summed up, the end result qualifies her to be his wife. But by implication, that feeling or wish or love of his is valid only at present since the future is unknown.

All marriages (majority of them let us say) that ended in divorce were once founded on love. The boy and the girl met and fell in love. While in that love, they cherished the thought that they would be husband and wife forever. Subsequently they put their thought into practice by actually getting married. But then later on, something somewhere went wrong, or did not function as had been expected. Or one of the partners or both became disillusioned. Or perhaps the wife became unfaithful to her husband. Or the husband turned into a brute or hopeless drunk. Or perhaps the wife did not have the most desired child. Or one of them, or both, became careless or driven into a crisis in which it became too difficult for him or her or both to observe the principal rules which make it possible for married people to coninue to live with and love each other.

In other words, love between a man and a woman in a marriage is, in many ways, a conditional feeling extended to each other and maintained on some definite conditions that are not usually mentioned at the altar. If they were mentioned, the marrying partner would probably deliver it like, 'Now darling, I take you to be my lawful wedded wife/husband (a), on condition that you will bear yourself out respectfully and strictly keep the present image of yourself that actually made me fall in love with you; and (b), as long as you will fulfil my expectations whatever they are.'

Why do people get married?

The commonly heard answer is, "Because they love each other.' But why, and how do people love each other? Or what is it that a person sees in the other so as to fall in love with that person? Is love an automatic thing that comes to you when you meet a person of the opposite sex when you are looking for a partner to marry?

Some people like to think that there is some kind of automatic spark that brings the two together. And if highly romanticized, they like to feel that they were born to love each other. But even if there was that automatic spark, everything about love usually begins from an ordinary situation. First, it is the eye of the beholder or the ear of the hearer that serves as the agent of that love. If it is the eye that secures the first contact, it is because the sight was a remarkable one. That is, at first, the eye captures something that is unlike all the others.

A common remarkable capture is brought about by physical attraction. A man or woman with a pleasant physical feature attracts a partner easier than one whose physical accomplishments are unpleasant. He or she is picked up quicker if he or she has a striking personality than the one with an unimpressive personality. A girl who has good education and employment has better chances of attracting men than one who is illiterate and unemployed. A man who is wealthy attracts more women to himself than one who is poor. All this is quite natural, but one could describe this form of attraction as a material one.

In other words, the cell of love is brought into being by various agents. Then that cell develops into complete love, so long as it comes into contact with other things; one of these may be the desire to have children. In this case, the girl who is a potential mother is preferred to the one who, by medical proof or otherwise, is unable to bear children. A girl who is lonely, or one who is too poor to support herself, looks seriously for a husband who is capable of providing for her needs. And that expectation by itself subscribes to her overall behaviour when she is looking for a husband. As she is so desperate, she would write her love signboard out in bold and colourful letters.

A prince has more admirers than an ordinary boy in the street. So, his chances of falling in love are more than those of the street boy. A princess is sought after more than a street girl. What does all this imply?

It means that people fall in love or let themselves fall in love for different reasons (motives too if you want). Some because of the desire for children; others because of loneliness; because of adventure, money, prestige, fear of single life in old age, beauty, profession, and so forth. For, if love was that unbiased, if it was that unconditional, if it was that institutional, indeed, beggars and rich people, the disabled and the able, the ugly and beautiful, all would be loved and cherished equally.

A man who falls in love with a girl because she is beautiful and, by implication, she would bear him beautiful children as well as boost his male ego, that man would be hurt seriously if that wife was severely deformed physically, or if she did not reserve that beauty for his bed alone; and he would be emotionally bruised if that beautiful wife did not give him children. The loss of her beauty is likely to kill his love or maim it terribly.

In other words, there are certain things that love cannot stand. That is, certain blows are fatal to certain loves. Love can, therefore, be nursed. If not properly fed and taken care of, it can suffer and die.

It does appear therefore, that love is not an automatic bonus that comes to anyone born. Rather, love is more or less an acquired syndrome.

What is it that makes people different from each other, because whatever it is, it must be responsible for the way people love? It is what they do mainly which makes them different. A pastor is conditioned by his faith and obligation to his God to think, act, and expect events in a given or authorized manner. A robber is forced by the game or rules of his occupation to uphold dishonesty and do his best to remain mysterious, as these are essential qualifications for his success in his life. A person who has been through a war assumes a different stance towards life, unlike one who has never been to a battlefield. A miser behaves differently from a spendthrift.

That is, people are as different as there are different factors to influence them. Because of their different likes and dislikes, ambition, education, cultural background, mental aptitude, past and present expriences, each person is basically different from the other. And of these differences, people are not equal—men and women. Surely, these differences have great influence upon the expectations and fulfilment of an active love between man and woman in marriage or otherwise.

When a girl has fallen in love with a man, the reality is that she has not fallen in love with just a man. Instead, she has fallen in love with an individual who has particular values and goals. That could be said too of a man who has fallen in love with a girl. What one person would love in another is what another person would hate; hence the proverb that one's meat is another's poison. It is then only wise for the girl who has fallen in love with that man to realise that he will expect her to tune her love to his outlook on life, profession, and belief. For where the person's heart is, therein lies the code of his love. It is from this standpoint that lovers appreciate and disappreciate each other; and the degree of success of their love, therefore, depends upon how successfully each partner matches the other in his or her expectations.

In accordance with the above discussion, the term 'my wife' for the individual man, stands for different things and values. Sometimes one is surprised to find a very handsome man married to a very ugly woman. Why should such a handsome man have let himself down so much, one wonders. Is it because, as often sung, love is blind and for that reason he couldn't have seen she was so ugly? The answer is yes, only if one forgets

23

that, that handsome man might have been looking for a different thing in a wife. Something else must have compensated her ugly features. Otherwise, all women do not mean the same thing to all men.

A man who is afraid of losing his wife to other men because she is beautiful, may develope a personal philosphy that it is better to marry a woman who is not very beautiful in order to keep her away from the claws of lady-killers. However, there are some principal things that any man considers in the choice of a woman for a wife; the leading being that she must be a woman; a woman biologically and a woman behaviorally. He expects her also to adequately perform the prescribed function of a woman. The gears of her personality, he expects, must be in consonance with his ideas and ego.

It is well known that no husband expects to be ruled by his wife; he expects to be her head and continue to be so regardless of what happens. His wife may want to see herself as the boss in the home and in her own way. But he desires to be and acts in a manner to make him feel that he is the president and his wife is the vice-president, of course, since no two presidents can occupy one and the same throne at the same time. Even though, liberally thinking, marriage is a partnership, that kind of partnership, and any partnership for that matter, constitutes a form of leadership and direction. For example, when a man and a woman are crossing a street with dangerous traffic, the woman expects the man to help her cross. By no means would the man expect her to help him cross the street unless he was sick, lame, or blind. Again, since it is the woman who conceives and bears children, that puts her in a definite role which automatically sets out the role of the husband in that marriage.

The husband may be aware that his wife has more brains than him but that does not, by all means, put him in a different position as far as their relationship is concerned. The fact that he can go to the kitchen and cook for her when it is necessary, does not make him a woman. His wife does not become a man simply because she has a paid job or talks in a deep voice like a man. Their love for each other is nourished by accepting their basic differences, which is best accepted or kept when respected and not questioned. So, naturally, the term 'my wife' and 'my husband' cannot be interchanged and any attempt to do so is fatal to the love that binds the two together.

Love is, therefore, a duty towards each other.

It is said that what God substracted from woman he put in man; and what he substracted from man he put it in woman so that both may seek each other eternally. Love and marriage to a woman means more or less a security for both her own survival and that of her own children. She comes to a man seeking, among the long list of requirements and expectations, physical protection. The presence of a man in her life assures her of physical protection. The presence of a man in her life assures her of physical safety although it is not always guaranteed. With a man in her presence, she is unlikely to be molested, raped or discriminated against on the basis of social status. For that reason, the signature of her marriage certificate is a weapon with which to defend herself. For her, the love of a is some kind of karate skill for self-defence. But it is not the physical protection that drives a man to marriage; this may be sexual security and the many other things which he can get only from a wife.

delivering a girl to a man for marriage. But not every woman is economically insecure. The girl with money will not let herself fall in love because of economic reasons, but because she desires permanent male company for her emotional needs, one of which may be sexual, the other getting children and so on. To this girl, unlike to the one who is economically insecure, dependency based on love and marriage is relatively circumscribed.

Does that imply that her love is, consequently, less blind than that of the financially insecure woman? This argument suggests that love and marriage diminish in their importance with increase in self-reliance. Part of what is called love is, for this reason, a basic need for material and emotional needs of the person. In other words, what tends to matter most in love is the received love but not the expected one. When a man does not appreciate what his wife gives him, that hurts the fabric of his love for her. If his love does not deliver the goods so expected of her, that damages the source of his love, and in extreme circumstances, it kills that love.

Love is, therefore, basically selfish. That is, it is not as blind as far as gain and security are concerned. And this argues strongly in favour of the idea that love that is unselfish is, more or less, imaginary or merely conditional. If so, could there be any truth in the claim, 'I was born to love you?' Can we still maintain that love cannot be shared? One can ask a more direct question, 'Is love born or created?'

Can love be arranged therefore?

The answer is, and very largely so, that love is born. But to say that it cannot be arranged is also to forget the many conditions and values that influence the love of man and woman in marriage. Hence, friendly love can also be arranged, increased or decreased, and can survive only if properly nourished.

It appears then that most loves, if not all, are not blind. However, if not all of them have 'eyes', which one is blind? Is it the one poets sing about—love that gives and gives and will never stop giving? Is it the one that knows no boundary? Is it the love of a parent for his child? Or is it the love of one's God?

But even the love of a parent for his child has limits. A child who picks up a gun to shoot his father should not expect that the father, however much he loves him, would be compassionate enough to let the child shoot him. He should expect the parent to react seriously in self-defence. The natural law that governs this is that man, if not all living beings, operates on the basis of self-preservation.

A parent who does not give his child parental care is said to have no love for that child. It cannot be said that he has love for that child merely because the child is his biologically. To be his properly, by implication, he must care. In that way only, can he be said to love the child.

To love, therefore, means to give. Love that does not give is blind love because it does not envision its implication. But the word 'give' is a relative word. The giving that makes love survive healthily should then be a generous one so as to generate thriving conditions for that love. We said earlier that love is a duty towards the loved, but we need to qualify this by saying that, love is much more a duty towards the object and much less a bonus to the subject.

In Christian theology it is said that God is love. And that God loves all people. And that all creations are God's, which would imply that he loves them all: birds, snakes and scorpions, trees and stones. But how would that love-for-all his creations exclude Satan from the loved? In that theology, too, it is told that God shall punish the sinners and destroy Satan. Or rather, he will destroy those who disobey him.

Does that make God's love, too, conditional like man's? Oh yes, otherwise there would never be mention of heaven and hell. The founder of Christianity, Jesus Christ, is reported to have said of love that one should love one's enemy. Then how does one love one's enemy when love is conditional? To what extent should that enemy be loved if the word 'loving' is a relative word? Under what conditions should the enemy be loved? Whoever enemy that is, if he must be loved, it is obvious that he should be loved under conditions that, too, must draw a limit. This is because all loves, like all things, have and should have a limit.

In this context of Christ and loving one's enemy, it is argued that when Christ said that one should forgive a wrong doer not only 7 times but 70 x 70 (4,900 times), he did not say that one should forgive a wrong doer a million times. And when he said that if one slaps you on this side, give him the other side to slap too, he didn't mean that you should allow that slapper to also kick you in the stomach.

So, there is no such a thing as love that forgives *always*. If it forgives, it watches over the behaviour of the forgiven. Love is blind, therefore, only when you overlook the limits and essentials of love; in which case that love becomes a distructive, substantially harmful and useless love.

Since love has demands and conditions that must be observed, when some of these conditions have not been respected, particularly the principal ones, there is bound to be disagreement. The only way to avoid such conflict would be to abide by the principles of love. Unfortunately, the ability to carry out these rules is not everybody's gift.

Ability to perform a duty depends upon a number of things one of which is interest; but interest to perform something is based on one's values. A man who feels that women are a stumbling block to his ambition will assume a stance of intolerance towards women as a whole, his wife prominently featured. A woman who thinks that she should have got herself a better man, assumes a frame of mind that is conducive to divorce. And since issues that make people appreciate life are of such a wide variety and cherished only at the individual level, when a marriage does not sympathize with the choice, that marriage asks for termination.

Disagreement in love and factors of divorce, are therefore, naturally incorporated into love itself, and any attitude of mind that regards divorce as unnatural, does not, obviously, understand the dimensions of love fully.

Since love is then primarily based on the current values and the vibrations of the courting couple and their feelings for each other at the time of marriage (usually with little or no knowledge of what to expect in the future after the wedding day), and since the couple is also vulnerable to the natural calamities and changes in values which may erode the very pillar that supports the marriage as a whole, it is only wise to give in to separation or breaks when there is no other way to sustain that love. It is not the will of the madman to be mad: it is not the fault of the short-range thinker to see things the way he sees them; and, incidently, those are good ethics for making law and punishment. Love is only love when given to the right person with the right vibration; or else, untuned love is crude love, with shaky prospects.

The African idea of love, away from philosophy, is ambiguous and diversely rich to embrace a much wider understanding and tolerance of one another. It goes beyond the eye, physical features, and sex, being an emotion that is deeper and richer than marriage itself and that can be expressed by words, being non-directional, joining the living and the dead, past and future. Polygamy, therefore, is but one expression of love in Africa, not an end in itself. Therefore, those who frown at it and wish to subject it to banishment are those who do not understand the dimensions of survival fully and are given to artificial judgments quoted from the examples of the man and woman walking in the street hand-in-hand.

CHAPTER THREE

The Whiteman's Polygamy

There are many Blacks and Whites who think that there is no polygamy or polygyny in America and Western Europe. In Chapter One I brought into focus the form of polygyny called consecutive polygyny. In the Whiteman's world, tradition and law, when a husband wants a second wife, he divorces his first wife in order to clear the ground for the second wife. If he wants a third wife, he divorces the second to make way for the third, and so on. And the White woman engages in polyandry by divorcing her first husband to marry the second; divorcing the second to marry the third, and so on.

Simply because the husband lives with one wife at a time, it is thought and claimed that the Whiteman's understanding of love is better than the Blackman's. Perhaps it is merely the definition or terminology which exonerates the Whites from polygamy. In America and Western Europe, there are two forms of relationship which may be said to constitute polygamy. One of them is that referred to as consecutive or serial polygamy, and the other one is what is commonly baptised or styled as 'Mistress' or 'Lover.'

In the latter, a man keeps one so-called legal wife with whom he lives under a common roof and name. She is licenced by the state's law to acquire and maintain his name and interests, authorized to appear or be with him as and when both wish to do so, and wherever they want to go. By virtue of this licence which is referred to commonly as 'Marriage Certificate', she acquires a new designation—Mrs. This designation or title is an endorsement for her to hold claims over her husband's property and to freely bear children with him. The property, material, and children from such union are, consequently, designated 'legal'.

If however, the husband of this Mrs is dissatisfied with the Mrs and so feels or believes that another woman could play a supplementary role, he schemes or goes out secretly looking for another wife, or rather an 'off-licence' if not illegal wife. Since divorce may result in some economic and social disaster, he decides to keep his licenced wife. The second acquired under these circumstances is popularly known as 'Lover' or 'Mistress.' Having fallen in love with the Mistress or Lover, the husband and the new 'wife' agree to a conditional marriage under the following terms:

1. The law should treat her as a second-rate married partner, and time may also come when such union or marriage may be illegal in favour of the woman accorded with the marriage contract. For that reason, she should see and perceive or regard herself as no more than a secret wife.

2. She should always try as much as possible to avoid any physical, verbal and other kinds of contracts with the first wife and, please, she should try to understand why.

3. She should never be seen in the streets with him, holding hands with each other shopping. Any such move is classified as a felony and is punishable by the holder of the marriage licence. Hence, the second wife should appreciate that it is a great honour and privilege for her to be associated with a man who lives and sleeps with another wife under the same roof. And as a result, she should be contented with the crumbs of bread from the table of the first wife.

4. She will, by all means, have no legal claim whatsoever over his social life and property; and acknowledge that the objectives, wishes, and aspirations of the first wife are superior to hers.

5. She becomes his second and secret wife on condition that she never gets a child from him. And in the event of getting one from him, either by her secret design, deception, reguery, or accidentally, such a child—male or female—shall be, by state law too, an illegal child; hence, a second-class child who shall be known in public places and in records as a bastard.

6. The bastard shall have no material and social claim over the father.

7. She will not be entitled to enjoy the company of the husband's relatives and friends; and the husband shall always be at liberty to ignore or hide from her relatives and friends.

8. She will have no rights whatsoever, nor shall her bastard, to use his name in public.

9. Only the holder of the marriage licence shall exercise unlimited privileges over the husband. The privileges of the husband over the second wife will be limited by the demands and capacity of intakes of the first wife.

10. The understood but unsigned contract of the second marriage stipulates that, at any time and place, the husband shall reserve and enjoy total liberty to walk out on her without any notice and liability whatsoever.

The bastards from such unions grow up as shameful, second-class citizens, usually abused by relatives and the public, misunderstood and treated with a high degree of rejection both by the public and the law. They are inferior, in as far as social life is concerned, to the children of the licenced marriage. The husband in such a marriage is always ready, at any time and any place, to deny the existence of such a marriage and any children from the union. He always endeavours to wear an innocent face in public and to adopt a behaviour that asserts that, indeed, he has one and only one wife. The tenure of such a marriage is often coloured heavily by a great amount of lying and sophisticated pretence to hide his true feelings and nature.

Such unity is classified by the man's faith and understanding of God as a sin; hence, the children from such union are children of sin and, therefore, a disgrace to the Whiteman's God even though in his theology he is told that all people, the bad and the good ones, are creations of God.

The Mistress is a public disgrace. She is treated by the public with maximum suspicion particularly by the licenced woman; she is discriminated against, abused and misunderstood. In domestic socio-economic politics, she is classified by the licenced woman as a 'husband thief', who deserves to be hunted down and eliminated even by extermination from the life of the husband. Her position in the society is insecure. The church sees her not only as a sinner, but an embarrassment although her failure to secure a licenced marriage was not of her own making. She is, therefore, a lonely person. So is her bastard.

This kind of polygamy is responsible for a host of psychological cases in the Whiteman's country. What happens to a human being who is not accorded respect and acceptance within her or his society? It is this system which, at its very best, manufactures suicide, hate, crime, pride, paranoia, worship of material things, male chauvinism, marital arrogance and woman abuse, obsessive jealously, blackmail, prostitution, just to mention a few of them. These are the typical characteristics of the Western civilisation.

Since the family is the nucleus of any civilisation, it is obvious that there can never be a worthwhile or complete civilisation unless its individual families rest on a secure and solid ground. Any civilisation, is judged by how it treats its children, women, widows, the old, the sick and the unfortunate. The majority of western families are weak and are breaking up speedily. The bond between man and woman in marriage, has more or less lost value in many homes in the West. Divorce rates are so high in most of the techno-societies, says Alvin in his book *Future Shock,* that a new distinct social group has emerged—those who are no longer married or those who are between marriages.[1] There are many parents who preach what they don't practise. VD is out of control. Use of terrible drugs is rampant. Mental hospitals are full of dying and wrecked people. Too many places are overpacked with criminal institutions and cities are unsafe for anyone to work in. Too many people have no natural affection, and in some places, homosexuality is defended by the church and government. Years ago, the family used to stick together; but nowadays there are countless family members who are enemies of one another.

Yet, hundreds of thousands of White men, both missionaries and government advisers—and others, of course—are in Africa today trying all their best to deliver the African from what they still consider as a primitive practice—polygamy, or rather African polygamy. And in the misguided belief that he is modernizing, the African is adopting the western marital law at the cost of his own civilisation.

Today, the primitive polygamy of the West has started eating into the African social life in large pieces. Is the African polygamy coming to an end to give way to the western one? And if so, is the western marital law suitable for running the African homestead? These are serious questions that should be answered by the African policy maker.

CHAPTER FOUR

Faithful Husbands: Do They Exist?

Even though today marrying couples do not make any verbal or written declaration with regard to faithfulness to each other, sexual faithfulness is so much implied in their marriage contract that discovery of an extra-marital love affair later gives a real shock. But such shock could be avoided by exposing unmarried people to some fundamental human behaviour of the married world, so that when the husband decides to enter into a second marriage, his wife would not be shattered.

There has been some unnecessary romanticizing of marital faithfulness. Today's world is endeavouring hard to bring us up with the thought that sexual frustrations and dissatisfactions end with marriage. It is a belief that does not tell us that marriage is not an end in itself, but a beginning of another life with new and similar frustrations. A girl who has been brought up to feel that she is 'self-contained' as far as marriage requirements are concerned, gets shocked terribly when she finds out that her lawfully wedded husband has taken a sexual course other than what she was brought up to subscribe to. Hence, the coming of the second or third wife in today's society is connected with infidelity. No wonder it raises many bitter quarrels and disappointments. Most girls brought up in such idealized world have resolved the polygamy problem by sweeping it under the carpet.

The aim of this chapter is to examine the sexual content of married life, to see how rich or poor or self-sufficient it is with the hope that such knowledge will aid us to understand or to assess the argument that men raise to the effect that a single marriage is not always sexually sufficient for the husband. The chapter takes a leap from traditional Africa into the modern one. This approach highlights the psychological factors that should help us understand the past married couples better and why traditional Africa treated sex with such generosity.

The word 'faithful' is a broad term. When used in connection with marriage or the relationship between man and woman, it connotes sex.

Hence, a man or woman who is faithful to his or her marriage partner does not, strictly, have any sexual relations with another person outside that marriage.

Sexual faithfulness between married people is considered a virtue. It is usual for every married partner to expect his or her partner to be faithful, sometimes even against many odds. As to whether that expectation is fulfilled, is another matter altogether. The saying, 'My husband is faithful to me,' (said by extremely few wives I believe) makes such beautiful music. But why should it be sung only by a few wives if any? There are many reasons. Indeed, you could dramatize it by saying that there are as few faithful husbands as there are virgins; that is, if faithful husbands still exist in this adulterous world.

What makes a person faithful to his or her partner? What kind of people make faithful husbands and wives? What circumstances, physical and psychological, make a husband or a wife faithful or unfaithful? Is it a lot of love and devotion for each other? Does faithfulness signify sexual satisfaction? And does unfaithfulness, therefore, symbolize sexual dissatisfaction? Or to raise a radical question, why should a husband or a wife be faithful to his or her partner anyway?

There are many questions and answers, general and ethical, that surround this subject. The general statement heard often that men are unfaithful to their wives and, therefore, should be condemned, is a serious allegation that could lead to a lot of misunderstanding. Or the husband who thinks that his wife ought to be faithful to him (even though that is what should be expected of her) may be making a rather too epensive demand. Not to mean that, of course, husbands and wives are supposed to be unfaithful to each other. A lot of fidelity and infidelity depends upon many other things.

Let us start off by appreciating that all married men had had some amount of sexual relations prior to their marriage. Most married women, in their girlhood, had their own experiences too. It is extremely rare to find a young man who is a virgin, if the term 'virgin' can be applied to men. But it is possible to find an adult girl who is and remains to be a virgin until the time of marriage. I am not being outrageous to say that men tend to be more promiscuous than women right from the beginning and to the end of their lives. In Africa and elsewhere in the world, the young man who is about to get married, has had sexual relations with another girl or woman.

That girl too, in many cases, has had sexual experiences with another boyfriend, bachelor or married. What this means is that most weddings are made by people who have had sexual relations with partners other than the ones they are marrying. The term, 'faithfulness,' in this case, can only be applied to the period of the union following the wedding day.

Some of the people have had so many sexual relations and experiences, in some instances bitter ones, that they consider marriage a salvation. And once they are out of the hook, they are determined never to return to that kind of (free sex) life. A man who used to suffer frequently from VD or other sexual diseases during his bachelorhood due to sleeping with all kinds of women and prostitutes, might have been driven to marriage by sheer fear of those bitter experiences. This husband will, where possible, act faithful so long as he can get reasonable service from his wife. His faithfulness would not be the result of great love for his wife, or of some religious values, but purely of personal security and he became wiser by settling down to marriage.

On the contrary, a man who had been a successful and beloved playboy, who had slept with all kinds of beautiful girls and important women but never had any bitter experiences with them, is likely to have developed a complex and expensive sexual requirements. Each woman he had taken to bed was, indeed, an experience by herself and a booster of his self-importance. Today, naturally, he would resent terribly being tied down to Grace because Grace cannot be Rhoda and Rhoda cannot be Fatuma and Fatuma cannot be the minister's daughter. A man with this stance is incurably promiscuous. In other words, the playboy has become spoilt; his wife should be better informed!

You must have heard of men's popular expression, 'change of diet' in connection with sex. A man who used to be free to choose his diet from the broad world, is likely to regard as prison the confinement to one woman in the name of wife. Marriage gives him a 'claustrophobia' and he would like to leave the doors to that marriage open. Living with one woman makes him feel like a person who used to be wealthy but has become poor. However beautiful or loving she might be, it will be so difficult for the wife of this 'gourmet' to tame him. He is not the kind of man who sees every woman in his wife. He will feel like a caged bird in her house and, however well-fed he might be, he would still long to fly out freely to enjoy the smell and honey of every flower in the field.

Then there is the case of the man who had lost his dream-girl, a girl who had looked too wonderful to be true. Gradually or suddenly, through death or otherwise, he lost her. Maybe she drifted into the hands of another man. That kind of loss bruised him badly. Later, after crying his bitter tears, he met another seemingly good girl. Even though this one could not measure up to the charm of the lost girlfriend, she was good enough to be his wife. So he married her in the end, but without, at any one time, forgetting his dream girl. But even after his wedding the latter, he is subconsciously still looking for the lost girl. This is the kind of husband who is likely to fall victim to any comparatively beautiful girl as he sub-consciously tries to recover his lost girl.

His love for the first girl may not have been on in-depth knowledge of her: perhaps, he had never had enough time to know her and discover her vices. Or it could have been an infatuation inspired by her physical beauty that seemed to promise paradise on earth. If he had lived with her for a longer period, perhaps she might have lost that glamour and become an ordinary girl. But time was too short and she went away as a perfect girl in his mind.

A man who has lost such a dream girl, goes out looking for the same girl in other girls. The same thing would happen to a girl who has lost a dream boyfriend; she would go out looking for him in the men she meets. He may think that, at last, he has found his dream girl in this Dorothy. Should Dorothy be a victim of the same psychological misfortune, she may also finally feel that her former irresistible Tom has resurrected in this Moses. So, the two—Dorothy and Moses—bind themselves with the joy of having found each other. As a result, they get married; but in actual fact, psychologically not marrying the real persons in each other, but marrying the ones they had lost.

Later, after living together but failing to find the dream in their marriage, they become very disappointed and disillusioned. This disappointment is likely to manifest itself more prominently in the husband. However much the wife becomes disillusioned with her husband, she realises how practically difficult it is for her to go out and continue with the hunt for the dream boy, not unless she was an Elizabeth Taylor or Princess X. But the man still has the opportunity, simply by virtue of living in a world where there are many women chasing few men. His disappointment, therefore, is more or less a new challenge to try harder to get his lost dream.

He is hopeful that, this time, he will get it in his next love.

This is the kind of husband who is difficult to please. The face trying to please him (that of his wife) is not the right face! This face was a mistake and that mistake should be corrected. He has no patience for this face.

He can easily plunge the marriage or himself into worse problems if, while subconsciously trying to recover the lost girl, he runs across a woman who is, in several ways, close to the lost girl. This new find will, most likely, wreck the marriage and the worst will enter his life if, by any chance the new find happens to be a devil in beautiful features. The only other thing which may save his marriage (that is, if he is still apprehensive of the new find) is having a patient, loving, faithful and, most of all 'understanding' wife.

The number is big of husbands who deviate from the glorious path of monogamy and fidelity by falling into this psychological trap.

One of the commonest things which make a husband unfaithful and drive him to another woman is sexual dissatisfaction, factual or illusionary. Many wives do not understand the rationale behind this. The assumption of the ordinary wife is that, since she is ready to receive him sexually when he wants (only when she is in a position to do so by some physical or emotional facts) there is no reason why he should not be a contented man. The usual question asked is, 'What is it that he is going to get from another woman which I don't give him?'

Putting this together with what we said earlier regarding some cases of higher sexual requirements in men, it should be noted that even though physical attraction is an important sexual requirement for a man, men usually enjoy sex much more when it has a touch of romance and submission. That is, the manner in which the woman carries herself, the way she walks, laughs and reacts sexually, the degree of her submission (or aggressiveness in some perverted cases), the feel of her body, her personal hygiene—all these contribute greatly to a man's sexual satisfaction. For example, it has been argued by many men that a beautiful but nagging wife is less likely to satisfy her husband sexually than a gentle, submissive prostitute. The fact that a man sleeps with his wife often does not mean that he is sexually satisfied. The high frequency of sex may simply be brought about by extra-romantic factors, for example, over-productive glands or psychological attempt to overcome some external frustration; or unavailability of a better (imaginary or factual) woman and so on.

Most men are vulnerable to women who are gentle, feminine, clean, forgiving and unegocentric. A proud, tough and militant wife should not be surprised when her husband is found with 'some low-class thing' or 'cheap' woman, regardless of his social status. Many wives have been stunned to find their husband having affairs with their maids—what they describe as 'unheard of'. Or the husbands simply ended up making the maids their second wives. The difference between the nagging and proud wife and the maid, for example, is that the latter does not question the integrity of her master the way his militant wife does. The 'strong' wife has also been known to hold her husband's sexual requirments at ransom and that is the surest way to send him, and any husband, to another woman be she a maid or a prostitute, or to the thought of becoming a polygamist. His move may not be an ethical one; it may not even be a wise one; but then that is how human nature is—emotional sometimes.

The other woman may enter his life through the door of hobby. The husband without something to occupy him outside his working hours may easily develop the 'dangerous' hobby of taking his bored life to women and, of course, to drinking. And as they say, where there is alcohol there is bound to be sex. He would be less promiscuous if he had a positive hobby such as reading, gardening, painting, writing, or if he was engaged in a second-income work, which keeps him away from thinking about women and meeting them.

Nothing is also more certain to send the husband to another woman than a wife who is careless in her personal hygiene. There is no amount of love, religion, or tolerance that could tie a man down to a smelly wife. Some women need more cleanliness attention than others. A woman whose sweating glands are over-active, needs more frequent baths than the one who hardly sweats. There are women who can go for days without taking a bath yet do not smell, whereas others start smelling a few minutes after bath. Others have extra-strong smell during their periods, no matter how much precaution they may take. It is not always true that fat women smell more than slim ones. A lot of this depends upon the individual woman's biochemistry.

Most prostitutes are very careful about their personal hygiene and overall appearance. This is because they have discovered what assets they are to men, and that if they are immaculate they can easily snatch the husband of the dirty and unimpressive wife. The husband of the dirty wife may want to be faithful, may hold a religious belief of fidelity, or may be a man of high morals, but the sexual odds are against him. Although men are susceptible to romance and fantasy too, most of them woud want to stick to their wives sexually. This is mainly because, apart from the moral obligation, there are many dangers that surround extra-marital affairs: fear of diseases, self-abuse and a bad name, and economic implications. But there are far many sexual imperfections in their marriage that force them to break the marital fence and take risks. It is not true that men cannot be satisfied sexually. They can. The challenge for women is how to do that; a tidy, neat, gentle, active, and permissive wife may be more successful in stopping her husband from going to another woman.

There are certain professions that also make it difficult for a man not to seek sexual relations beyond his marriage. These include those that take the husband far from his wife and demand long stays, or those with irregular working hours. A man who works in the night and sleeps during the day when his wife is already out in the field or in her office, or one who works far from the country home where his wife lives, has a sexual problem. So is the sailor, the soldier, the man employed by an international body who has to keep on travelling from one country to another. Travelling men meet all kinds of women (single, widows, divorcees, and married) and are often thrown into situations of social interaction that are more conducive to infidelity, concubinage and poly-gamy than to marital faithfulness and. monogamy. Vocational and professional trainings that take men far from their wives could, very well, introduce the 'good' husband to the 'bad' behaviour: concubinage and polygamy.

To present this analysis is not to justify or approve of such unions. Whether or not we caution the married man against involvement in any secondary union, that does the least to change human behaviour. The girl singing the marital vow at the altar should be aware of these difficult situations that await her lawfully wedded husband and get used to the idea that, practical living will be such that, from time to time as the turn of events shall dictate, she will be forced to share her lawfully wedded husband with other invisible and even visible women. No one can give her an easy solution regarding how to avoid that problem. Most marrying men come to the marriage determined to keep it monogamous and they think that it is possible to be faithful to that marriage. But then, as the saying goes, man proposes and God disposes; what they learn later on or what life forces on to them, makes them disillusioned. All that should be said about it is that this problem (if it is a problem at all) should be left to the individual husband to solve it in his own way. A religious man for example will have a different way of dealing with it.

The husband's unfaithfulness as we have seen, may be influenced by circumstances that stem from his wife. The wife may be aware or unaware of her fault. Or it may stem from his past life: his fantasy, his profession, his psychological frustration and so on. The other woman may, therefore, be an element built into the very material upon which the first marriage stands, and it is too cheap to blame either the husband or wife as being the cause of the second union.

There are, no doubt, some faithful husbands here and there; but this is not necessarily because they are such wonderful husbands with super-will powers. Their fidelity or monogamy might have been forced onto them by some circumstances of physical, psychological, economic or religious nature. Or they might have been very lucky to get the right partner for marital fidelity and monogamy. Or they might be living in situations that are more conducive to fidelity. For example a man who is married and lives with his wife in the bush teaching, in a place where there are no mature girls and other loose women, is forced to bring his sexual return forms to his wife for signature, unlike a married teacher living in an urban setting where he interacts with all kinds of women. Naturally, the tolerance of the two teachers towards their marriage would be quite different, and their wives face different challenges in their marriages; hence, environment has a great influence over the quality, content and endurance of the marriage. And above all else, fidelity or infidelity can be a condition of the mind.

CHAPTER FIVE

Polygamy for Today and Tomorrow

Polygamy is very much alive in Africa today. Whether or not it is on the increase or decrease, is a different argument. There are, and yet will be, thousands of couples who find, and who will find it a useful and moral form of marriage. Polygamy is usually hit hard by economic difficulties. For sure, the economic grounds on which traditional poly-gamy was founded, are changing rapidly. The move from nomadic life, then from agricultural to industrial setting, is definitely the single most influential factor. Industrialisation and urbanisation, in particular, have introduced very fierce accommodation and administrative problems. The lowly paid urban worker with consequently poor accommodation can no longer afford a permanent second wife. The cost of bringing up children and educating them have to be given priority over marital conveniences. It looks as though the wind of change is in favour of the western form of polygamy and increase in the hit-and-run extra-marital relations.

But economic hardship is nothing new in Africa. In traditional Africa, not every man could afford a second wife. Judging from the geneological records most men had only one wife at a time, a few commoners had two wives, and only in exceptional instances would one have three or more. The last category was found as a rule only among members of the royal families as well as other important or wealthy men. In some special cases, such men could even have several tens of wives.

Keeping more than one wife in traditional Africa also meant working hard to maintain them and to undertake additional responsibilities. There were also the bride gifts to be paid for each wife. No wonder it was the well-to-do man who could afford a bigger family.

Considering the means of acquiring material things, the amount of bride gifts paid was quite high. In the Akamba custom, for example, the 'payment' (if one has to use that term) averaged 48 goats, 2 cows and 2 bulls, several 'drums' of honey, and a great deal of consumed alcohol and foodstuff. A rough translation of that into modern monetary terms may give us a better picture:

48 goats at Ksh. 250 each	9,600
2 cows at Ksh. 1,500	3,000
2 bulls at Ksh. 2,000	4,000
2 'drums' of honey at Ksh. 1,000	2,000
consumed food and alcohol appr.	3,000
Total in Kenya Shillings	21,600

A round figure of Ksh. 22,000 would not be a small amount to pay for a man with a low income. Again, traditionally, the husband is supposed to provide each wife with her own accommodation and private property such as cows for milking and a *shamba* on which to grow her crops. Again, translating this into minimal monetary terms, we would get the following picture:

1 private home	20,000
4 cows at 1,500 each	8,000
2 bulls at 2,000 each	4,000
10 acres of land	80,000
Total in Kenyan Shillings	112,000

We shall assume that the bride gifts of the first wife have been paid and she has been provided with a home and some property for a decent start in the countryside. In most parts of Africa the climate is hostile to farmers and a 10 acre piece of land is small although the same size of land would be substantially big in places where the rainfall is excellent and the ground is fertile.

From the above, hypothetical scenario the man must potentially have about 135,000 shillings to start a sound marriage: that is, the cost of the bride gifts plus the cost of accommodation and some property. To get himself a second wife, he would have to go through the same exercise. Two wives would cost him 270,000 shillings. That would rule out many men from the game and force them to be contented with one wife.

One may argue that in the past, land was free and that the cost of living was quite low, so polygamy could not have been that expensive. But we can answer this with: is it easier to acquire property today than it was in those days? Even though bride price has been abandoned in some quarters, that does not make polygamy any cheaper, considering the economic responsibilities of today for keeping a family.

Following the footsteps of tradition, if the marriage has to be meaningful and respectful, each wife married today must have her own accommodation and private property. There are many men who are economically strong to give each wife her own home and property. Some can even afford a car for each wife, a country home for one wife and a city one for the other wife. So, to reject polygamy on the economic reason that it is too expensive does not hold merit at all in as far as some people are concerned. In modern times, there are some men who are as wealthy as they want to be and are in a position to afford any number of wives. If they can do so, shouldn't they be free to be polygynists?

We cannot yet dismiss polygamy as inapplicable today on any basis. Of the discussed reasons responsible for polygamy in traditional Africa, namely, childlessness, wife's bad health, sexual incompatibility and so on, many of them are still very alive today, with the exception perhaps of 'labour force' in some limited instances.

There are couples who cannot accept a childless marriage even today, so the door for the second wife is still open. Invalidity, sexual incompatibility and inequality, widows, and men who are still charged with a moral conscience to marry the girl they have made pregnant—all are still with us today. These are enough reasons to make polygamy still very relevant today and tomorrow. The 'containers' in which African polygamy was stored, have barely changed from being 'gourds' to become 'bottles', and the brew still remains quite African. After all, living in cornered homes, wearing sunglasses, drinking wine and speaking English or French, can not make the African lose his Africanness.

CHAPTER SIX

Objections Based on Christian Religion

Unless the general reader is interested in the Christian view on the issue of polygamy, this chapter exclusively addresses itself to the person who is a Christian and has been told and converted by the western interpretation of that Bible to believe that polygamy is a thing of evil men. Christianity has played an enormous role in shaping the mind of the modern African. Many governments, powerful and influencial institutions of Africa today are headed by Christians or persons who are sympathetic to Christian values. It would then be a grave mistake to discuss the polygamy issue without touching on the Christian view.

In spite of the African's desire to learn the truth regarding the real biblical stand on the polygamy issue, church leaders have denied him an honest examination of the issue; questions which he would have raised about the subject were easily suppressed as thoughts inspired by the evil spirit. I therefore thought it would do the Christian reader good service to give him that honest view.

One of the greatest arguments against polygamy in modern Africa was brought to Africa by White missionaries; obviously, an argument based on the cultural values and western interpretations of the Bible. To be a Christian, goes their claim, a married man must have only one wife. The deduction made by this is that polygamy, even as was practised by the big names of the Old Testament, must have been against the will of God.

This reasoning is mainly based on the interpretation of Apostle Paul's speech and Genesis 2:24. Paul's speech comparing the love between husband and wife to the love between Christ and the church, quotes Genesis 2:24 and adds: 'This is a great mystery and I take it to mean Christ and the Church (Eph. 5:32). As a husband leaves his father and mother in order to cleave to his wife and become one flesh with her, Christ left his father, when he was born man (Phil. 2:7), his mother, when he died at the cross, and cleaves to his bride, the church, and becomes one with her as the one head to the one body (Eph. 1:22-23) in an exclusive relationship.'

From this speech the western theologians see nothing else but a firm statement that Christ came to abolish polygamy. A further proof of this claim is obtained from the famous classical argument in support of monogamy as deduced from Genesis 2:24 which is part of the account of creation. This verse is read to mean that life in the Garden of Eden depicts monogamy as something intended by God from the very beginning. The reference to 'man' and 'his wife' (not his wives) becoming 'one flesh' is all that is responsible for this interpretation.

If we took the message from this angle, the account would surely imply that there is a man to every woman born. Or that there is another man, a bachelor of course, to marry the woman who has been divorced, or one who has lost her husband through death. Considering the evidence on the ratio of sex distribution that we discussed earlier, one would therefore wonder what kind of confusion the God of creation would be introducing by his failure to make sure that every sex born has a corresponding and destined partner.

It is also ridiculous to expect the Genesis account to have used terms other than singular ones in reference to marriage. What should we understand by the statement, 'Man is likely to destroy his own life in this world'? Of course, the term 'man' here does not mean only one male person. It means the human race. The Genesis reference to 'a man' and 'his wife' cannot be literary taken to exclude any polygamous union and much more in that emphasis because polygamy has always existed among and practised by the most prominent biblical names; in fact, the biblical God's most beloved men were polygamous, namely Abraham, Jacob, King David, Solomon, and so on. How come that their God did not condemn them for their plural marriage? Could they have practised polygamy against the wish of their God, and is there any evidence in the Old Testament to support such a claim?

Abosolutely none.

Was theirs a different God from that of our present Christians? Again, no, for 'I am the Lord, unchanging' (Malachi 3:6). If the coming of Christ had something to do with changing the marital law, he would have been very clear about the issue because it is an extremely important one. He would probably have said, 'Please, the God of Abraham and Jacob has changed his mind about polygamy. So, verily, verily I say unto you, be monogamous if you want to inherit the kingdom of God.' Instead of saying something to that effect, Christ chose to remain completely silent about polygamy, for we can hardly point with certainty to a single verse in the New Testament where he condemned polygamy or even commented on the practice in a manner to decree it for his followers. If anything, his teaching on marriage was limited to his affirmations of its insolubility. Neither was the issue treated directly and explicitly by the New Testament writers who, quite often, naturally under the cultural ethos of their particular time and place in history, accepted monogamy as a normal point of departure for any discussion of marriage.[2]

If implications were to be considered in passing judgment on the issue, one might like to refer to the question put to Christ by Sadducees, 'Master, Moses said, "If man should die childless, his brother shall marry the widow and carry on the brother's family." Now we know of seven brothers. The first married and died, and as he was without issue his wife was left to his brother. The same thing happened with the second, and the third, and so on with all seven. Last of all the woman died. At the resurrection, then, whose wife will she be, for they had all married her?' (Matthew 22:24-29).

Here one would like to ask some questions: Were all these brothers still bachelors? Was it not possible that one of them or several of them were married? Was this not an opportunity for Christ to have commented on monogamy or polygamy had it been such an important issue? He could have said something like, 'Look here fellows, this is against the will of my Father'.

When Christ said, 'I tell you, if a man divorces his wife for any cause other than unchastity and marries another, and anyone who marries a woman divorced from her husband commits adultery' (Luke 16:8) did he justify consecutive polygamy as a better evil than simultaneous polygamy which can be justified biblically by the statement 'What God has joined together, man should not separate' (Mark 10:9)?

How then did the Whiteman develop this Chrstian dogma against polygamy? Polygamy was never a widespread practice in the cultural area where Christianity took roots and developed during most of the past nineteen years, testifies a Catholic theologian, Eugene Hillamn[3]. Polygamy is really an alien custom to the peoples who make up the vast majority of the Christian population in the world of today; they therefore, have relatively little to say directly and explicitly about this custom. Greco-Roman attitudes, practices, and conceptions shaped the understanding and the structures of Christian marriage, even as these very attitudes and conceptions were themselves being influenced by Christianity. The central notion, for example, that Christian marriage is constituted by consent comes directly from Roman Law and particular historico-cultural practices and conceptions that gave rise to the law. The use of the ring, for example, as a symbol of betrothal and later as a sign of the contract, comes directly from the pre-Christian Roman practices[4]. Pre-Christian Rome also provided the Church with a ready made formulation of the purpose of marriage in order to bring forth children[5]. Moreover, it was the traditional pagan 'religion of the hearth' *that directly inspire the original Greco-Roman view that marriage is both indissoluble and monogamous.* From this same socio-religious source also came the various norms still used by the church today.

Theolegians who grew up with this background and who were to operate in Africa where the socio-religious stand was different, had no option but to preach their own views and, confronted by the polygamy issue, they had just to try to justify their view by holding on to any biblical straw in their support. It is not surprising therefore, says Lawson, that Canon Law's basic principles and obligation of the marriage contract seem to be similar to, if not identical with, Roman Law[6]. For our purpose it is particularly interesting to note that Christianity did not introduce monogamy into Greco-Roman world[7]. As the result of the pagan religio-ethical conception of marriage and famiy life, monogamy was already present as the only legal form of marriage; and polygamy was already proscribed for Roman Citizens when Christianity was just coming to life in the form of that culture.

As regards the Jews Josephus, the Jewish historical writer of the first century, mentions in two places that polygamy still existed among his people and Justin Maty, also gives witness to the existence of simultaneous polygamy among the Jews of that time[8].

The legal monogamy insisted upon by the Greeks and Romans (who are the founders of the western thought) was often supplemented with institutionalized concubinage and widespread prostitution, and divorce was a recurring problem[9]. In the Roman world at the time of Jesus the marriage rate had declined so seriously that registration was enacted to penalize the unmarried. And in reaction against the prevailing conditions in Rome, the Christians insisted upon the pure monogamy of Greco-Roman tradition; and, perhaps to some extent over-reacting, they exalted celibacy over marriage, which they seemed to value mainly as a remedy for concupiscence.[10]

Today, celibacy is still regarded by a good number of the western Christians as ideal for Christians; hence, the widow or widower is expected to 'die' sexually; or those who are unable to obtain sexual satisfaction from their first marriage, should practise celibacy rather than give in to polygamy.

Although polygamy existed among the Jews until the 11th Century, it had been abolished as early as the 4th Century by the Roman power who ruled the Jews; but that abolition had absolutely nothing to do with Christian virtues. As for Africa, polygamy remained an honourable form of marriage until the coming of the White missionary armed with his cultural ethnocentricism and a theology that perceived marriage in a Christian view endorsed by the Greco-Roman Law of marriage.

In no record does Christ condemn or ban polygamous marriage as he so strongly preached against the Jewish practice of divorce. There is no discussion in the New Testament regarding what a man with several wives should do if he wants to be a Christian: whether or not he should divorce the other wives and remain with one before he can be baptized as had been decreed by the early missionaries to Africa. Neither is there any statement addressing itself to co-wives. Apparently, the only explicit statement is the one that requires a bishop or elder to be 'faithful to his one wife' (1Tim. 3:2; Titus 1:6).

Augstine and other Catholic fathers did however, admit that polygamy was not rooted in the Bible, but in the Roman custom. 'When polygamy was a common custom,' says Augustine, 'It was no crime; it ranks a crime now because it is no longer customary. Now indeed in our time and in keeping with Roman custom, it is no longer allowed to take another wife, so as to have more than one wife living'.

No wonder therefore, the strongest objection to polygamy has been systematically championed by the Catholic Church. One would have thought that by now such foreign customs as discussed above would have been distilled from the Gospel to make the Gospel pure, but, it looks true of the Roman customs too that, traditions die-hard. Much so when this

Objections Based on Christian Religion

particular custom is still included in the spiritual menu of the head of the Catholic Church, the Pope.

The Pope, who could as well be described as the king or president of the Catholic Spiritual Empire, wields powers that are unproportional to those of anyone else we know of in the spiritual world. The question often asked by people outside the Vatican State is: Who has conferred such powers upon him and under what biblical interpretation?

Since the Pope, in his power, endorses the dogma that forbids Christians to participate in polygamy, it is necessary to include him in this discussion. In order to gather evidence with which to approve or disapprove of his claim, we must look into the spiritual content and legitimacy of his institution, historically and biblically.

The Pope is referred to in the superlative degree of piety as the Holy Father—the infallible head of the Catholic Church. As such, what the Pope says is deemed to be or interpreted as the word of God, since he and God share the quality of being free from sin. In 1984, during his Eucharist Congress in Kenya, Pope Paul II reiterated the Catholic's stand on polygamy by condemning it as a practice that directly beguiles the glory of God which was revealed from the beginning. 'In the Old Testament,' said the Pope, 'polygamy was sometimes tolerated, but in the new covenant, marriage was restored by our Saviour to be a communion of one man and one woman.'

He was simply telling African polygamists and others that they lived in sin and, as the result, they would never see the Kingdom of God which is reserved for only monogamous Christians in as far as the married population is concerned.

What is a Pope?

For the interest of the general reader, it is important for me to define what Pope means. In any case, it should not be assumed that everybody knows who the Pope is. Firstly, not everybody is a Catholic Christian and; secondly, not everybody is a Christian and thirdly, Christianity is not a subject taught to everybody. To a Moselm, the term Pope may be as equally dubious as the Aga Khan to a Christian.

The Oxford Dictionary describes the Pope as *The Bishop of Rome as the chief Bishop of the Roman Catholic Church*. The other question asked by many people is why the Pope is designated 'holy'? Or rather, who and what makes him holy? But these are questions only asked in the dark background, if at all, by a Catholic Christian; otherwise, there is a big stigma attached to questioning the Pope's authority. In the first instance, such questions are seen as implying doubt or disbelief in God. It is so rare, better say unheard of, for a person to stand up in a church during a sermon or discussion of some biblical chapter and ask, 'Excuse me please, why does that God let people die of hunger or be killed by others?' It is assumed that those who come to church have absolute belief in the existence of God and that they understand everything told to them and for that reason there is no need for questions. Any challenge on the Pope's designation and whatever he says as a spiritual leader therefore, must be seen in this light.

Unfortunately, it is the nature of people to doubt things and to ask questions. Many people, even those who profess Christianity and kneel down to pray from time to time, still wonder at times whether there is a thing called God; or if God exists, how he works, thinks, not to mention where his dwellings are and why he has always remained invisible to man.

Answering the question regarding the holiness of the Pope, I see no reason why I should hesitate to say that the designation Holy Father is a man-manufactured one. The question why he is called Father is another issue altogether. Christ referred to God as 'My Father'. The Catholic Father is deemed to take the position of God in the interaction with people. The Holy Father in question is a man without a wife and, by implication, childless because he does not indulge in conjugal love.

The state of being unmarried and of celibacy for priests is not an order from Christ or God. Jesus of Nazareth, whom the Christian doctrine is based on, is not recorded to have said anything about celibacy. It is assumed that he himself did not get married even though from his age of 13 to 33, his records (the ones that are known up to date) are completely missing, and no one knows for sure what this son of God did with his life during that time, whether or not he fell in love and married and fathered children. The strongest that is presented in this regard is the argument that if he was married, his family would have featured, at least, in his trial.

The earlier priests and popes were married and had families. Pope Sergius III, for example, even had a mistress. Her name was Marozia whose mother was Theodora, the wife of the Senator who lived some time in the 10th Century. His illegitimate son with Marozia became Pope—Pope John XI (931-936 AD). Marozia was fertile in producing Popes. Alberic II the Pope was also her son. Then the nephew of John XI, son of Alberic, grandson of Marozia was raised to papacy at the age of 18 by his uncle John, but he was deposed in 963 AD after having proved very immoral.

As it is obvious from the above case, even the papal throne has not been innocent. It has suffered from corruption and nepotism. And this also applied to other priesthood promotions. And it became so bad that finally the Catholic authorities, the synods as they are called, were forced to impose celibacy upon priesthood in an attempt to stop this nepotism as priests would now not have children on to whom to bequeath their positions. One of the earliest compaigns by the synods to decree celibacy upon priesthood took place in 410 AD, where the synod of Selucia united the Persian and Greek churches and decreed priesthood to be celibate. But the war against marriage for priests was not completely won until the 12th Century.

In 1074 AD at the Council of Winchester in England, for example, when the Pope declared celibacy for priests, he issued an order that priests must not divorce their wives; and further, to stop them from extra-marital affairs, he ordered them to take the oath of faithfulness to their wives. However, William the Conqueror dismissed the Pope's order and told his English priests not to recognize the dictation. But the matter was taken up more sternly by the next Pope, the first to be elected by the people, Pope Gregory VII the Great, who banned clerical marriages and excommunicated married priests. In his *Dicatus* Gregory put it all to a full stop by decreeing that only the Roman Pontiff was to be the universal Pope; hence banning the use of the title 'Pope' by any bishop. Then he decreed divorce of wives married to priests.[12]

To be excommunicated by the Pope in those days was a grave thing. Some of the victims went through cruel tortures, were hanged and burned; and some died in chains suspended over a slow fire. Papacy had become a power to reckon with; and its might kept developing from strength to strength. Augustinus Triumphas (1240-1328 AD) for example, declared, *All princes rule is subject to the Pope who can remove them at pleasure. No civilian law is binding if disapproved by the Pope. The Pope can be judged by no one, and no one can appeal to God against the Pope.'*

As early as the 5th Century, it was declared that there should be no more public confessions, and that only confession to the priest should be the order.

As the Pope developed into a figure of worship, so were his 'things' taken as holy items to be worshipped. Mary, the mother of Jesus, was given the title 'Mother of God' in 451 AD. Her statue, therefore, had to be worshipped. By 709 AD, the kissing of the Pope's food had begun. And nearly 80 years had to elapse before the church authorized the worship of the cross, relics, and images. The real worship of Mary was established in 788AD. Two years after that, the worship of Joseph, husband of Mary, was instituted.

However, not every Christian was in favour of this image worship. A controversy is presented, for example, by one priest, William Sawtree who is recorded to have said, 'Instead of adoring the cross on which Christ suffered, I adore the Christ who suffered on the cross.'[13] His punishment? He was burned. After which the clergy was forced to guard against such insurgencies by styling the Pope *not as a mere man but a true God (1401 AD)*. However, all did not sail smoothly with these orders. There was widespread appeal to abolish priesthood celibacy besides prayers for the dead, offerings to images, and transubstantiation, the doctrine that the bread and wine in the Eucharist were changed into the body and blood of Christ. People appealed against auricular confession, the whispering of one's sins into the ear of the priest.

Over the years, there were squabbles to reduce the Pope from a God to a human being. It wasn't until the 15th Century, for instance, that the papacy was transformed from absolute constitutional monarchy to one regulated by the legislative body. But even after that, the Pope remained an exceedingly powerful person. In 1670 AD the Vatican Council established Papal infallibility by a vote of 5,133 to 2. In simple language: the Pope was declared incapable of making mistakes or doing wrong—holy, that is. Now with his infallibility declared, his opposers had a case to answer. That was the year, in England, during which 10,000 people were excommunicated and sold as slaves in the colonies.

But the struggle to make the Pope a human being survived. In 1870 AD, the Vatican Council met again over the issue of infallibility and reinforced it, defining the Pope's duties as immediate and unlimited in every part of the state. The Pope was, and is voted Holy, therefore: The Holy Father. The infallible. When one politician referred to Jesus Christ as 'good', Christ is recorded to have denied the credit by saying 'Why do you call me good; no one is good but God alone' (Luke 18:19). But the Pope is not only good but holy!

The Catholic Church, led by this infallible person, is traditionally plagued by problems of corruption. A tip of this iceburg, has been seen in the discovery that Pope John Paul (Albino Lucian) was murdered by the Mafia and Freemason occupants of the Vatican City. The Vatican City is an independent state, hence a law unto itself. It measures 108.7 acres in size. The Pope, flanked by his bachelor cabinet ministers of cardinals and bishops and nursed by spinsters commonly referred to as nuns and sisters, is the head of over 800 million Catholic Christians of the World—nearly a fifth of the global population. The behaviour of the Vatican City is not much different in administration from any other secular state we know of today. It has its diplomatics, foreign policies, local interests and, by all means, it is a highly commerical body with its own banks, doctors, universities, schools; controlling interests in companies in the fields of insurance, steel, financing, flour and spaghetti, mechanical industry, cement; shares in General Motors, Shell, Gulf Oil, General Electric, Bethlehem Steel, IBM, TWA, the Italian giant building SOGENE firm, and so on. Its commerical interests are not confined to the seemingly 'harmless' fields; for it owns shares also in some firms that manufacture items ranging from nuclear items to the Pill. The history of the Pope and the Vatican Financial Empire and its tentacles hardly give it the image of the holy kingdom it seems to claim from the public. Women are banned from the higest echelons of the Church (by implication because they do not possess Godly qualities); yet, all has not been well with the office bearers. Whereas a good number of the priests have contained their emotions with success, quite often, one comes across illegitimate children fathered by Catholic priests, mistresses supported by them, and prostitutes who are their customers, not to mention another lot of homosexuals and lesbians. When Pope Gregory ordered that all married priests should divorce their wives, it was with the feeling that (it still survives today) woman was the stumbling block to Christian faith.

If the papal throne is holy, infallible, and the Pope himself a God who can forgive man's sins and condemn polygamy, that is good for Roman Law traditionalists and Euro-ethnocentrists, but it is not biblical and African.

Most of the African local churches, save the independent ones that have sprung up recently, are replicas of the western theology and have been very active, too, in condeming polygamy. However, others have decided to keep silent about the issue, or simply sit on the edge between the West and Africa.

A good number of the independent churches, which are seen by the western church as protestants of the 'true' Gospel, have got rid of this hang up and pronounced that polygamy should be allowed by the church and given Christian blessing.

Even in recent times when some western churches were pondering whether or not to bless the marriage of homosexuals and lesbians (they do marry them nowadays), these same churches could not understand why a widow should marry the husband's brother who has another wife and get church blessing, leave alone receiving baptism which the Catholic Church, according to the constitution of Pope III, is a privilege of the faithful. The African independent church seems to have the right vision in as far as this issue is concerned and it is in a unique position in Africa to make the necessary reforms.

There should be no reason why a man who wants to marry a second wife in a mutual agreement with the first wife, for instance, should not be married in the church with full respect. There is no reason why a pastor cannot be a polygamist if he so desires or if the conditions rule that he be one. Is there any reason why the African church should not encourage good and respectful polygamy as a means of giving marital happiness to the unmarried women? Is there any reason why women married to polygamists should not be accorded full church respect? One single and lonely woman once put it this way, 'Dear God, if you did not want me to marry a polygamist, where is the single man that I was destined to marry, for I am weary of waiting for him?'

Since the western church has the economic knife and yam in her hands, the radical African church that is waiting for the support of the western church, should get used to the idea that there is not going to be any Dollars, Pounds, German Marks, Francs and so on from the wounded Roman Catholic bank account and that, no more Catholic gowns shall be worn to promote the African belief on matters that the Vatican City does not respect. 'But then,' cried one of the members of the independent church, 'fotunately, an inspiration to the believer, the God we worship is also a wealthy God, loving and understanding; so, there should be no reason why his cheques to us should not be payable to us directly instead of passing through Europe and America for endorsement. It is a good feeling to know that our God can communicate with us directly, without whitemen-go-betweens. This is and should be the beginning of Christian revolution and reform in Africa. We have the capacity to take care of ourselves spiritually."

CHAPTER SEVEN

Considering Polygamy

For whom the polygamy bells toll

That one's meat is another's poison explains the dimensions of human differences and personalities. It is nonsensical, of course, to advance the claim that polygamy is wrong. Good questions to ask are: To whom is it wrong? Or under what circumstances does it become wrong?

To say that it is wrong, obviously, is to assume a definite stand in evaluating cultures and human values. In fact and in all fairness, all that one can and should say about polygamy is that it is a way of life that, under certain conditions, becomes meaningful to some people, but gets disapproved of by others.

The truth is that in certain situations, normal or abnormal, there are women who do not mind, or who are bothered the least about giving themselves to a man as a second or third wife. That is, she does not see anything wrong in being a co-wife. Or if she can perceive the dangers of marrying a polygamist, the risk of going through life unmarried outweighs the pains of being a second or third wife. The reasons that lead to this decision are many and one cannot attempt to enumerate them here.

Likewise, there are men who cannot get used to the idea of being pinned down to one woman they call a wife throughout their life. Again, the reasons are many, physical, psychological, social, economic and otherwise.

So, if there is a woman who is willing to marry a man who is already married to another woman, and if it is possible to find such a man who would enter into such a union while retaining his first wife, who am I to her to tell her, 'No, sister, that is wrong!'? And if there is a man who believes that his life would be a complete waste if he did not take a second wife, and he was in a position to actually secure that second wife, who am I to tell him, 'Don't, that is immoral!'? All that we can tell a person looking for a second marriage is, 'We hope you know what you are doing, that you are aware of the responsibilities and costs involved in the move. There are XYZ factors that contribute to a successful polygamous marriage.'

The aim of this chapter is to set the pros and cons of polygamy. People who condemn polygamy are those who live a privileged life, just like people who condemn divorce are those who mainly enjoy healthy marriage. That, generally speaking, a man can get married at nearly any time in the stretch of his life, and that the chances are always there that he can get a willing woman to marry him (sometimes at the lift of his finger) indicates the privileged position in which men live. However, a woman's world is not equally blessed.

In so many cases, a woman cannot get a man to marry her at any time, and that unfavourable situation becomes much more grave as her productive period diminishes. In Africa, at least, marriage is very much tied down to producing children. A girl who has gone beyond her fertile period finds it extremely difficult to get a man to marry her. Her productive period is, unfortunately, not spread out over most of her life like man's. In order to beat time or to catch the 'children' train before it is too late, sometimes she is forced to consider taking any transport that comes sometimes at great risk as long as she does not feel that, by so doing, she is not committing suicide.

How does the single, lonely girl or woman see these things? Of course, this does not mean that all single women have a common mind. However, nearly all of them have a common problem. That of finding a man to marry or, at least, give them company. Nuns and others, some of whom are 'devotedly married' to their profession and others who hate men or are lesbians, have something to live for; but not the single, lonely woman who feels that life has no meaning whatsoever without a man to marry her. What is true of life is that all women cannot be nuns; some women have to be mothers in order to bear nuns, as nuns have not, except in peculiar cases, been known to bear and bring up children.

In traditional Africa, all female persons were born and brought up to get married and have children. There were extremely few cases of single women, if there were any at all, who remained so up to the end of their lives. As marriage was a cornerstone of social security, it was not merely any man who could attract women for marriage. With the social security in mind, a woman was likely to go for (and her family was likely to give her to) the man who appeared responsible, kind, and gentle. Such a man was not always the unmarried. In so many instances, he was a married man already.

When that responsible man expressed interest in having a second wife, then there were many women at their disposal. Or else, when all men seemed to be married, the marriage door was not closed completely to the single woman. Traditional values also played a great role in the single woman's view of marriage. What made some women desperate to get married was that, first and foremost, marriage was a social status. Single life was therefore not only feared but abhorred for what it stood for and promised to the future of the bearer. Among many ethnic groups in western Kenya, for example, if such a single woman fell sick and died, she had to be given an elaborate burial that could only be seen as a shame.

The feeling that the single woman could still get married in a single or polygamous marriage, gave her psychological relief. Even when all her colleagues had disappeared into marriage, she knew that all was not lost and eventually, she would find her own home.

Today, there are some married men who are still equally responsible, kind, and gentle, interested in or forced by situations to take another wife. And somewhere in the world, much so in Africa, there are single women who are desparately looking for such men. Why then should they not meet?

Of course, this brings in the position of the first wife which falls into risk by the coming of the second wife. It is understandable that she stands ridigly against the coming of the second wife for many reasons some of which we shall mention later. But, it is quite fair to say that not all married women resent having a co-wife, particularly when there is a plausible reason behind it in so far as the security of the home is concerned. The truth is that, in the Africa of today as well as that of yesterday, and also elsewhere in the world, there are many married women who have the capacity, or who see and appreciate the reason for sharing their husband with another woman.

Some of this has been culturally cultivated. Cases are known where, for instance, the first wife would go to the extent of forcing the husband to marry a second wife and she would raise hell if her request was turned down. Such was the case among the Samia where tradition dictated that once one's first born got married, it was a great shame for the mother to continue to sleep with the father in the same house.

Whereas some of these traditions are dying out, there are still cases in which the first wife encourages the coming of the second wife because of one of many reasons. For example, her husband may appear to spend most of his time with that woman out there where he also seems to spend most of his money; or if he goes out to sleep with all kinds of women and risk the first mariage with a sexual disease; or as in the case of some communities a child is fathered outside the marriage but is automatically brought to the marriage and has to be taken care of by the man's wife. In such situations, the wife may feel that it is much better for this man to marry a second wife.

Although many negative things can also be said about the other wife, polygamy has its many positive sides too. For instance, it has been observed that men with more wives tend to be more industrious than monogamists. This situation, of course, has an economic basis that the demand for protection and supply in this home is higher than in the home of the monogamist. This increased demand throws great challenge to the able man who now tries his very best to satisfy that demand. But perhaps one of the most precious contributions of polygamy to the first marriage is in averting a divorce in the first marriage in a situation where the first wife and the husband cannot stand each other any longer. In that case, both the mother and her children are spared the psychological pains that accompany breaking marriage.

The story of men who love being surrounded by many women either as wives or secret lovers, is not new. Many men of great achievement are sexually very active. History is full of such men, be they kings, great artists or businessmen. There seems to be a link between sex and man's success. Men who have accumulated a great deal of fortunes and achieved outstanding recognition in literature, art, industry, architecture, and profession, argues Napoleon Hill, were motivated by the influence of woman. The emotion of sex is an irresistable force against which there can be no such reaction as an 'immovable body.'[14] Such irresistable force may not necessarily be the quality of the first wife; it may be the other wife or lover who is responsible for that inspiration.

One of the big problems of monogamy is that of one of its partners taking the other for granted. It is much more damaging to the marriage when it is the wife who adopts this attitude. She may feel too sure of her position in this marriage because she is the only one who holds the sexual flag of the marriage. Or she may feel that, because of what she has contributed to this marriage and what she is, the husband cannot, really, manage his life without her. Or she may bank her security in this marriage on one of her accomplishments which may range from physical beauty, economic strength, social status and so on. For that reason, she may feel that there is no need for keeping herself on the run to maintain an efficiency expected by her husband. Accepted that the husband may also nurse similar feelings towards his wife and even at a worse level, it is in the nature of man-woman relationship on the planet in which we live, that the man tends to get away with most murders. And since it is the man who is more dangerous to the stability of the marriage if disturbed, it is only too advisable to explore all the areas of compromise in order to save the marriage from any disaster.

The second wife finds a competitor in the first wife, claims a polygamist, and the first wife finds hers in the second wife. Each tries to outdo the other in terms of service and creativity. In other situations, although these are very rare, both wives form a strong team, working together. If the first wife knows that number two is very hard-working and hygienic in her cooking, to ensure that her husband continues to come to eat her food and enjoy company with her, she tries harder to upgrade her performance, or she takes the challenge of being more original and inventive. That is, each wife learns from the other and is motivated by the other to higher performance.

This may sound as if the aim is to keep the wives on the run, competing for the husband's appreciation; but should that be the interpretation, one should not also forget that the husband is equally kept on the run by the wives in order to please them. Such challenge can have its positive side to the husband too. Driven by the force to please his wives, he is injected with super power to perform even better. Sex transmutation contains the secret of creative ability, adds Napoleon Hill.[15] Destory the sex glands, whether in man or in beast and you will have removed the major source of action. For proof of this, observe what happens to any animal after it has been castrated: a bull becomes as a cow after it has been altered sexually; that is, sex alteration takes out of the male, whether man or beast, all the fight that was in him or her.

But does he really need a second wife?

My argument does not concern itself with the issue of the third, fourth, and fifth wife and so on. It is centred on the first and second wife. There is the saying that the first wife is a necessity but the second one is a matter of convenience. The second wife is, however, the point of departure from the commonest form of marriage namely, monogamy. In the Akamba tradition, the family has the obligation of helping the son, materially and otherwise, to acquire his first wife; but they keep away from any 'costs' involving the son's effort to marry a second wife.

Any form of marriage, monogamy or polygamy, is a serious commitment. It does require absolute confidence to make a decision to get married, most of all, because marriage is a move that affects the life of the individual in a big way and in so many ways. So, naturally, this decision should be taken with maximum clarity of what one is doing and, over and above, with a knowledge of what such a move means in terms of responsibilities, emotionally, economically, and socially.

Since this discussion is not meant to be only for those who are already married and those contemplating a second wife, it is good that we broaden the scope of the discussion by also examining some practical issues that are required by a polygamous union. This is in appreciation of the view that the book will also land in the hands of a bachelor and single girl who have always wondered whether or not polygamy was something they could go for one day. But to get to the second wife, we must pass through the first wife.

The coming of the first wife

A couple gets married bursting with every hope that everything in their union will proceed as planned and that their love will combat all marital problems. But it is so usual that after the wedding of the two who are so in love, that they discover sooner or later that this thing called marriage carries with it too many other things and liabilities. And some of the things involved are so difficult or complex or demanding that, in some instances, the question of their love for each other is put to great trial.

They discover that there are many other things unconnected to the emotional feelings that they have for each other. The first child usually arrives in the midst of other anxieties, such as those connected to work, unexpected misfortunes, responsibilities related to relatives and friends, complications in emotional adjustment to each partner, and so on. All those find their way to the love-ship.

When a young man is courting a girl with all those endearing words, looks, and romantic letters, he may not be aware that, that darling of his could, one day, turn out to be selfish, intolerant to his friends and relatives, unfaithful and a cheat, argumentative, irresponsible parent, a bad cook, careless in her personal hygiene, a terrible gossiper, bad tempered, extravagant, and so on, in addition to being susceptible to health dangers.

During that courtship, all that he sees and feels when she is with him, is love and eternal happiness. He can hardly visualize that one day he will get extremely angry with her, quarrel and fight with her and call her names. Nature has a way of tucking all the unpleasant things about her into some place out of his sight and smell. That is why it is so exciting to fall in love. Nature has blindfolded him and she is telling him, 'Take this girl: she is the most wonderful thing in this world: I can assure you nothing will ever go wrong between you and her.'

When a seed is ready for planting, nature gives it the mechanism of locating a place in which it should plant itself and germinate, then grow into a plant. For a fruit seed, nature provides this mechanism by covering the seed with sweet flesh to attract an agent to pick it, eat the flesh and in so doing, transfer the seed to a different place away from the mother plant. In the case of that agent being a human being, as he eats the sweet flesh, he appreciates the value of the fruit and thinks of growing more of such fruits for himself. Hence, he goes and plants the seed. In the case of animals and birds, the fruit is swallowed for food and by so doing, the seed is transfered to a new ground. This is seed dispersal, as we learn in biology.

This same mechanism can be seen clearly in the multiplication of the lives of the human being. That thing called love and its consummation is comparable to the sweet flesh of a fruit and the act of eating that fruit. As they 'eat' of the contents, they create circumstances that make new ones come into being. In other words, the force that brings a man and woman together, is no more noble than the biological dictation that enables the seed to find a new ground.

A poisonous fruit is also capable of having attractive features to lure an agent into picking and eating it; in the process its seed is transfered from one place to another and given ground for growing. Same with the human being. A bad man or a bad woman, is capable of producing qualities that are attractively woven into a mysterious thing called love. And nature has always hidden the poisonous part of the person inside the person, just as she has always succeeded in hiding it in a fruit. This should be an important observation in the understanding of love and marriage and human motives.

To fall in love does not mean that those who fall in that love will get on well with each other. Even in the parable of the fruit, not all that is attractive to eat and that which is eaten is good to the health of the eater. Marriage based on the idea of love alone is an idealised one. The idea that those who have fallen in love should have a warrant to get married and continue to satisfy each other is a thing that makes good music and religion to the less emotionally mature persons. A healthy marriage decisions must, therefore, be based on the acceptance and awareness of all those outside natural forces that, so often, stand in conflict with love. Once that idea has been observed practically, then the first marriage can be allowed to take place, naturally with room for modifications (through additions or subtractions) for the survival of that union. Such healthy foundation has been laid also for the second marriage as a redemption of a great fault or disatisfaction in the first marriage.

The coming of the second wife

The basic thing to understand is that a wife, any wife needless to say, is a human being; and a sound knowledge of human behaviour is a great investment in any successful dealings with human beings. To advance the defence that a woman is also a human being, should not imply in any way that in our part of the world the value of woman as a human being has been questioned. It is only a statement to lay down the foundation that, even though a woman somewhat looks and behaves different from a man, her basic requirements are those of a man. We can simplify this by saying that man is another version of woman; or both are the two sides of the same coin.

The basic requirements of a human being can be divided into three main parts.

1. need for food
2. need to be loved
3. need to be protected

These three; namely, food, love, and protection form the triangle by which human endeavours and achievements are measured and judged. What happens if:

(a) one's supply of food has been threatened?

(b) one's loveline of love has been threatened?

(c) one's protection and security have been threatened?

Anxiety may be one of the consequences. And the move to fight against that anxiety or threat, calls into use many forms of struggles which have their own results, good or bad. When the three basic requirements have been gravely threatened, extermination of the threatened life becomes a possibility of reality.

In order to present a more balanced argument, let us examine these three more closely. We can do so effectively by beginning to raise some practical questions, such as: 'What kind of food, love and protection does he or she need? Who is she or he? Where does he or she live?'

Need to be loved

When we are loved, or when we experience a sense of being loved, we feel secure. In the first place, we do not expect cruelty from persons who love us. Instead, we expect from them consideration when things have gone wrong, or when we have made mistakes. The feeling of being loved is an assurance that we are, indeed, important persons.

But that love given to us is not enough when it is not extended to other people whom we treasure most, as well as to other things that are valuable to us. That is, we expect those who love us to also love our relatives, and friends. Those who love us should also be sympathetic with out ideas, tastes, and pets.

64

Need for protection

We want those who give us protection and shelter to extend those to our relatives, friends, pets and be ready to defend our ideas. We want them to protect us physically and morally, and give us the feeling that we shall stand protected by them in the future; therefore, there is no need to worry.

Need for food

As we must eat in order to live, have good health and appreciate the joy of living, we want those who give us food to let us share it with our brothers and sisters, parents, uncles, cousins, aunts, friends, and pets.

Why?

Because it feels good to live with and among those who love us and those whom we love and appreciate. These are part of us and they make it possible for us to realise ourselves and the dimensions of the life we live.

The analysis of these three basic requirements makes it clear that, it is not the mere material love, food and protection that we require from those who love us; but both physical and spiritual support.

When a husband has provided his wife with physical love, food, and shelter, that is commendable; but they are not enough without his spiritual concern for her. The home may have all the food she needs—with security guards and music—but if she suffers from the feeling that these things are not hers permanently, or when she feels that an oncoming event might take away that love, home and security, she is bound to fight against that loss. Even though the question may be a good one regarding whom she should lose those things to and why, all that is overpowered by the instinct of self-preservation.

The coming of the second wife as a second consumer of the privileges of the first wife, or rather as a rival, should be seen physically and psychologically from this perspective. It is so obvious that the second wife is coming to subtract from the first wife regardless of whatever material benefits she is bringing to that marriage.

When a husband introduces the subject of marrying a second wife, the first wife is met with the direct challenge that her love, shelter, and food will be reduced from fullness into halfness. 'He will not be my husband any more,' she worries, 'but our husband.'

The questions in the foreground of this move are; Why should the husband expect the first wife to simply understand and even go to the extent of welcoming and appreciating the coming of the second wife? **What is it actually that the second wife is bringing to the marriage to strengthen it?** What is so noble about sharing his life between two wives? If there are no concrete benefits, or if such anticipated benefits are too obscure to the first wife, such husband should expect the second marriage to bring disaster.

A very important step is for the husband to seriously consider whether he really needs a second wife. The idea of having another woman to go to when the first one grows sharp horns or tries to be too smart, is an exciting and often an irresistible one to many men. 'Two is always better than one,' goes the saying. Not only in reference to polygamy but to nearly all things of life. However, with regard to marriage, a second marriage can be not only disastrous to the first marriage but to itself too.

There are many things that people think they need which they really don't. **An emotionally immature man is likely to be infatuated with** the idea of having another wife, when infact he lacks the ability of keeping two wives happy. The man contemplating a second wife must ask himself whether he can provide satisfactorily, physically and spiritually for two wives. The second wife, like the first one, is a demanding being who needs full attention: in short, she needs all the things that a married woman needs. If his desire for a second wife is based on some remote feelings or reasons that may not be intelligible to the first wife, it may be helpful for him to counter-check his intention with the opinions of other persons whose judgment is respected. To desire something does not necesarily make what is desired good to the one who wants it. Certain desires can be very expensive and dangerous.

Traditionally, the second wife comes to the marriage to solve a crucial problem in the first marriage. Even outside the ethos of tradition, the other woman is often courted because there are some disatisfactions in the first marriage. Is it merely the issue of the so-called love which is propelling him to marry that girl for a second wife? Is it her beauty alone that courts the second marriage? No. A sensible marriage, and particularly a second one, cannot simply live on physical beauty or on the hollow subject of love:

other deep factors must support the union if it has to survive.

With a good understanding of what a second wife means to the security of the first wife, traditional Africa invite the first wife to a dialogue relating to the possibility of bringing another woman to this home. She is then allowed to give her own evaluation of the situation. If the husband is loving and genuine, he has no option but to share his feelings with his first wife. He is not shy to face her squarely and tell her what he thinks and feels. It is during this discussion or debate that the wife has the opportunity to articulate the factors that she thinks or feels relate to the material and security side of her own marriage.

Today, this tradition of discusion should be recommended to those who seek a second wife. The method is a down-to-earth one, pragmatic, and an honest approach to life. At this discussion, naturally, the first wife would want to know:

1. Will the husband still attend to her physical needs after he has got himself another wife?
2. Will he still respect her as his first wife?
3. Is the second wife going to be an indirect replacement of the first wife? What reasons make such exploitation not possible?
4. What happens to her own property? Will she still have personal property which she can dispose of the way she wishes?
5. Is the second wife coming to inherit equally what the first wife and the husband have accumulated so far?
6. Is the second wife coming to share accommodation with the first one, or is she going to occupy her own home?
7. If the second wife is going to require her own home, how is it going to be financed—by using the savings or the material of the first marriage?
8. Is that other woman a person that the first wife can easily be related to? Will she respect the first wife in as far as the order and importance of the first marriage is concerned; and could she be made to promise that?
9. Is she someone with an income or simply a dependant who will live on the sweat of the first marriage?
10. How does the husband intend to share his time and responsibilities between the two wives?
11. Is that other woman willing to share a husband with the first

wife and, in a way, form a team with every member of the family to overcome the many problems that a polygamous marriage faces?

12. Who is that other woman? What is her background? Is she an honourable person or a mere pick from the mass who is bound to bring shame to the homestead?

These are very important issues that should be thoroughly discussed before arriving at a decision to get a second wife. This approach expels the first wife's doubts about the kind of insecurity the second wife is likely to throw into the first marriage.

If the decision to have a second wife is based on the first wife's infertility, there are some important points that must be given attention to. The first wife would find the decision acceptable (if she is generous) as long as there are some medical or obvious proofs that she cannot have a child of her own, and that it is not the husband who is infertile. Having waited for a few years for the child without success is not enough to justify another marriage. An important question to ask is, 'Can the husband have children with a second wife when he has failed to have them with the first wife? Any proof to support that claim if it is yes? If the husband is merely being impatient, the first wife is likely to oppose the move. Or if it is because he wants to have a son whom the first wife has tried to get and failed, there should be a good dialogue to weigh the pros and cons of the issue. For example, could adoption of a son solve the problem if it is possible to adopt one?

The first wife's fear is justified if she suspects that after the husband has got the child he wants from another woman, the first wife would diminish in her importance and all the attention and love would be given to the wife who has delivered the desired goods. Suffering from this fear, the first wife is likely to do whatever she can to frustrate the coming of any other union, or even try to sabotage it if it already exists. Her objection may not have anything to do with the child; after all even her child may bring relief and emotional security to the home. Her negative reaction could be motivated by the simple fact that she feels threatened in her marriage. The question that she wants answered practically is, 'Will you love and cherish me even when the other wife has proved herself better than me by producing the child you so desire?'

There is also the other catch in as far as having a son or daughter is concerned. Medical studies have shown that it is the man's sperm that determines the sex of the child. So, the failure to have a son should not be blamed on the wife, rather than on the husband. However, the problem is sometimes more complex than that. It is not unusual to find a couple who have been having a series of daughters having a son at a very late stage.

If marriage of the second wife is based on factors related to bad health of the first wife, the first wife needs to be assured practically that the good health of the second wife shall not eclipse her from the husband's love and attention. There is also another question to answer, 'Is the good health of the second wife going to be of any physical and emotional help to me as your first wife?' If the answer is yes, the means of implementing that should be discussed.

If the coming of the other woman is based on sexual incompatibility and inequality, this can be, indeed, a tricky and delicate subject for the husband and wife to discuss and reach a compromise. Women do not take easily or kindly to allegations of sexual inadequacy levelled against them. Any articulation of a problem of this kind is seen by the accused woman as an attack and a very serious one, against her personality. This is an issue that needs a very special approach.

Probably by the time the husband has started talking about a second marriage, the first wife has already an idea of whatever deficiency in the marriage, unless the husband had always kept silent about it and did not make any attempt to register any of his grievances to her. Whatever the case however, it is advisable to let the first wife know the problem. If it is merely sexual disatisfaction, who knows, perhaps she could improve on her performance. If it is neglect of her personal hygiene, the threat may shake her out of her carelessness. As the proverb goes, many people do not mind running as long as something or somebody is chasing them.

The move of the husband to inherit a widow, with all the good intentions and humanitarianism attached to the deed, may still be not such a welcome thing to the first wife. In some instances, the widow in question may be a staggering liability with which the first wife would not like to be associated. The problem with the average widow is that she has a family of her own that needs support; but that problem may also be watered down by other factors. For instance she may have a complete home and property of her own such that the coming of the caretaker does not create any more liabilities for him. On the other hand it may also depend upon what kind of a personality that widow is: she may be capable of creating disaster to the new home. But at first glance, one knows that generally the move to inherit a widow has many implications, biggest of all, the economic burden.

If the widow has a large family for instance, such would not fail to alarm the first wife; and much more if this husband has a small income. The classic question asked by the wife is, 'How are you going to cope with this additional burden and yet be available to me as and when I need you?'

It is dangerous for him to jump into the responsibility without a thorough discussion with the first wife. However, this is not usually a matter that he can undertake without the involvement of the entire homestead. In many communities of Africa, he moves in only with the request of the complete family and all issues pertaining to the widow's liabilities and assets and her position in the new arrangement, are thoroughly discussed.

The involvement of the whole homestead is highly commendable and should be encouraged because it contains the elements of solving the basic problems, and gives the new union a sensible direction and meaning. The first wife's immediate reaction against the coming of the widow is to assume a hostile attitude towards that widow which she may express indirectly or in instalments, and she may lay down impossible demands for her husband to meet in an attempt to force him to grind to a halt.

If the marriage is generated by the need to secure additional manpower, this claim must be endorsed by the first wife. The husband may just be trying to exaggerate the problem in an attempt to justify a second marriage. Perhaps the manpower problem could be solved by a better management of the existing hands. Have the full resources been utilized? Could an employee do the job?

The classic claim in connection with a second marriage is that the husband is looking for someone, '. . . who can take care of my property, who is responsible, and whom I can trust.' He therefore feels that a wife would be a much better person than an employee. Unfortunately, this claim has not been always correct and the husband realises this when it is too late after the damage has already been done.

If the second wife is coming to help the husband run a grocery that is growing fast, for example, while the first wife takes care of the farm, the second wife, believing that the property in the shop belongs to a corporation, may have little or no dedication in running such a business. She may feel that this man is simply taking her as another worker. Unless the foundation was properly laid down, she may feel that quite possibly a time wil come in the future when her services will no longer be needed and she would be dispensed with. With this kind of fear or suspicion, she may choose to employ a style of working that is against the spirit of the husband. She may also feel justified in spending the money the way she feels. This would be very much in support of the first wife's doubt about the usefulness of such a second wife.

If she feels exploited whether in reality or in her imagination, she would start pulling down the business. On the other hand, she may nurse the feeling that, since it is only she and her husband who run the business, the property involved should not belong to anyone else except the two of them and that the family of the first wife should be excluded. A terrible disagreement is likely to spring up from this stance particularly if the first wife decides to actively challenge the second wife's conviction.

What all this means is that, even though theoretically it may appear that the presence of another wife would improve on the business, successful implimentation of this would depend very much upon not only the emotional maturity of the wives involved, but also on the high quality of leadership of the husband, much more so because the expectations of the children of the first wife must always be considered.

Above all, before the husband brings in this new business 'helper' the first wife, who has a share in the business too, should be satisfied from the beginning that the second wife is capable or appears capable of performing the duties required.

If the husband has made a girl pregnant or has inconvenienced her gravely against her marriage prospects with another man and for that reason feels that he should marry her, the position of the first wife is clearly being tampered with and shamefully, by a matter related to her husband's infidelity. How does he justify his infidelity? The questions which he must endeavour to answer statisfactorily are:

(a)   How is that girl going to adjust to the marriage?
(b)   What are her expectations? Does she expect the husband to desert his first wife in her favour?
(c)   Is she willing to help the wider family in keeping the homestead

happy?

(d) What kind of affair did she have with the husband; and, is there proof that the child in question is the husband's?

(e) How emotionally mature is she?

(f) Will she simply make use of the opportunities and hospitality of this home then quit later when the dark clouds have cleared?

(g) What are her special qualities?

(h) Has she got an income?

(i) Is the husband really in a position to support another wife?

In the first place, the first wife may not say yes to a proposed second marriage mainly because doing so would be tantamount to accepting the husband's unfaithfulness. However, whatever means he chooses to bring her to his home, he should do his best in preparing the girl and his first wife for some better co-existence.

Generally speaking, whatever shortcomings the first marriage has which forces the coming of a second wife to the husband's life, must never be swept under the carpet. Those shortcomings should be discussed and faced however unpleasant they may be. As the saying goes: one does not cure a wound by avoiding to wash and dress it simply because the operation is painful.

The moral question of why the first wife should give in at all to a husband's desire to share him with another woman, is another subject altogether; but it might be necessary to summarize it by saying that really, there are only two choices at her disposal. One is to tell this husband to go to hell by way of divorce, if by so doing she would have solved her personal problem and would be assured of a strictly monogamous relation elsewhere. The other choice is to let him go ahead with the second marriage if he cannot do otherwise, then, of course, try to make the best out of what remains of her marriage. As the saying goes, if someone gives you a lemon, don't throw it away but make a lemonade out of it. The question is, 'Is divorce better than accommodating a plural marriage?'

Many women prefer polygamy to divorce. Those who can avoid polygamy by way of divorce and yet live happily thereafter, should be free to do so and, indeed, it is good for them; but surely, we must also appreciate the view of those who decide to keep the marriage for whom this book is written.

CHAPTER EIGHT

Approaching Polygamy

Approach to the Negotiation

The husband is contemplating a second wife: how does he introduce this sensitive subject to his wife? He would be courting disaster to simply go ahead and bring in another woman to the first marriage. Will the first wife understand or sympathize with the wish?

When she has decided to show no understanding whatsoever, or when she does not seem to appreciate the reason for the second wife, it is very wrong for the husband to resort to force. These are love matters and they succeed and bring joy only when they come through courtship. That is, as far as it is possible, the first wife should be courted into accepting, or at least, seeing some sense in the move. Force, like death, should come only when all the other efforts have been tried and failed.

Perhaps she resists the decision because of what she already knows about her husband's character. In this decision, she might be seeing an attempt to get rid of her indirectly. So, in order to convince her that his is not a bad intention and that she is still very secure, he might have to consider discussing the issue with her among other chosen friends or relatives whom she trusts and respects. Presence of other people as witnesses may dispel most of her fears which she is very likely to spell out in their presence.

At an advanced stage, a better move would be to involve a lawyer to make the terms of marriage of the first wife as firm and secure as possible. But this may not be practical because many men detest the involvement of lawyers in their marriage affairs, sometimes under the fear that the wife may like to articulate her rights legally from time to time during the many disagreements that accompany any marriage. It is felt best and encouraged that married persons should not communicate through lawyers, even though, application of law in marriage is not a new thing in African civilization.

In traditional Africa, law was not a responsibility assigned to an individual as it is today; there were no professional lawyers. The law of the people was a collective responsibility of everybody and that is why it was so difficult to deliver a corrupt judgement. In as far as marriage law was concerned, the lawyer role of today was assumed by relatives, friends, and neighbours. These were very much involved in the engagement and wedding of the individual. Every loophole was eliminated; indeed, nothing was taken for granted. During the courtship, exchange of the bride gifts, and the many eating-and-drinking-together parties, indirectly and naturally, the couple made every commitment. Any deviation from what the law expected, was corrected there and then. So that by the time the couple got married, they had already 'signed' the complete marriage declaration, and the papers were filed in the minds of the people for any future reference. The marriage certificate was an invisible contract in people's minds. Theirs was a scrupulous legal system which protected the rights of everybody

So, to involve a lawyer in today's agreement should not be seen as a foreign concept. It is only a modification of what has always been there. After all, the lawyer is not coming to tell the husband how to run the marriage. He is coming simply to help the two put things where and how they want them put, indeed, for clarity and smooth living.

In these days of diminishing powers of the big family and the clan, a lawyer is very helpful. If the husband's motive for having second wife is a good one, why should he not make it easy for his wives to know their territories thoroughly? Polygamy works out its worst when started off and made to function on unclear circumstances and doubt.

To avoid future problems, much more in the case of inheritance and other family rights, it is highly recommended that the three should sign a legal contract of some form. This signing can be carried out traditionally or modernly.

We have referred to this dialogue in relation to the first wife and husband. But there should be another substantial dialogue, if possible, between the first couple and the prospective second wife. It is very dangerous to take things for granted. In this dialogue, certain questions would be asked and their answers given. And it would be even better if, at one stage of the process, there are witnesses. From the prospective second wife, the first wife would like to know:

(a) Is this your decision to marry my husband or you have been lured into it?

(b) Do you know what it is to be a second wife?

(c) Do you think you could make a happy second wife, and what makes you think so?

(d) What position do you expect to be in, in this homestead—the number one or the number two wife?

(e) What will be your contribution to the overall family?

(f) How do you expect to start off—from the scratch or somewhere above?

(g) How do you expect to be treated by this man's first wife?

The prospective bride would also like the first wife to answer questions to the following effect:

(a) Am I, therefore, accepted; and is there enough room for me in this home?

(b) What do you expect of a co-wife in the maintenance of the family?

(c) What is the ceiling of my freedom in this home and whom am I answerable to?

(d) Shall I be your equal as a co-wife?

(e) Do I have my husband when the need for him arises, or will all the priorities be given to your requirements?

(f) With whom should I share my accommodation, and am I allowed to accumulate personal property?

Generally speaking, the position of the second wife in the family is a weak or shaky one. Though she loves the man and she may have poured out all her loyalty in vows she will have a hard time trying to learn how to swim in the pool of this family. Everybody in the whole family (including the children and relatives of the first wife) has his or her own expectations. Usually, she feels insecure. But where there has been a thorough discussion prior to the marriage, most of that insecurity is minimized.

To eliminate most of this insecurity, the bride would want this man to clear the air in the presence of his first wife by answering questions to the following effect:

(a) Do you take me as an equal of your first wife?
(b) Will I be exploited because of my junior position in this marriage?
(c) How secure shall I be in this family, and what preparations are laid down for my security?
(d) Will all my activities and movements require the stamp of your first wife, and if so, shall I be allowed to differ with your first wife?

It is very difficult to correct a polygamous marriage that started off with a bad foundation, particularly in these days when the magic of the extended family is not in force. The momentum of a polygamous marriage is greater than that of a monogamous one. This stresses the need to start off the marriage with as clear vision as possible. Husbands who do not pay great attention to this procedure are shocked when their wives start tearing each other out.

The dynamics of the extended family, in its positive contribution was in everybody's dedication to participate in correcting things when they went wrong for and on behalf of the solidarity of the homestead. There were many supervisory eyes. Human nature is such that we tend to work better and complain less when we are supervised and when there is always that feeling or awareness that there is a power behind us. That power was contained in the constructive spirit of the extended family.

Today, although many people still live in the extended family structure, the situation is changing fast; some families have changed dramatically already, or they can change suddenly so that the husband finds himself all alone facing his two or more wives and their children. When something goes wrong, he may have little help or none from the other members of his family, either because they are scattered all over the country and he cannot get them together to look into the problem, or because he has broken away from that family, or because of another modern constraint which could as well be economic. In this case, it is obvious that the modern polygamist has less control power at his disposal because of reasons dictated to him by modernity. The pressure of marriage, no doubt, lies much more heavily on him than it lay on the past polygamist. In the past, the slogan was *our wife*; today it is getting to *my wife* or *your wife*, so that the 'corpse' of your marriage is more or less your own to bury.

In anticipation of all these modern constraints, it is very necessary to let the second marriage kick off as neatly and honestly as possible.

Again, the fact that two women have been forced by circumstances to share one man for a husband, does not essentially mean they should like each other, or develop similar views and interests. The two may stand miles away from each other in their likes and dislikes. Sometimes so much that the only thing they have in common is the husband and his name. This is why he should acknowledge the hard facts that, if the marriage has to be successful, it should be based on a firm, clear, and honest constitution.

When no agreement is reached

It should not be assumed that the discussion between a husband and wife concerning the introduction of a second wife, must end in agreement or, in some form of compromise. Even when the wife has been fed with all the good reasons and facts in support of a second marriage, she may still stick to her 'no'. She may know too well that she has permanent bad health which makes it impossible for her to carry out the full marital obligations, yet something from within is telling her that she must say 'no' to the marriage.

This behaviour may be due to an inner fear that, however helpful the co-wife is likely to be, she, the first wife, is signing the death warrant of her own marriage. Reasons alone and even persuasion may not convince her, particularly if she is motivated by selfishness and short-sight.

In the case of a deadlock, usually the husband has the upper hand. Many husbands simply go ahead and implement the decision by marrying. This, of course, amounts to dictatorship; but whereas dictatorship is not a good way of doing things, there are many instances of life when such course has to be taken: that is, when all the other alternatives have failed. Too bad for the wife, but then not all her fears are founded on truth, and any other attempt to please her may be disastrous to the whole marriage.

Further Basic Requirements

When a man is thinking of becoming a polygamist, he may get carried away by the seeming convenience that the other marriage would offer that

77

he overlooks certain important things. He may not even stop to do a week's homework to find out what the evils of polygamy are, for, indeed, they are there. The coming of the second one calls for a good number of responsibilities the main ones of which are:

1. Additional accommodation.
2. Additional children to the family.
3. More emotional burden over the husband.
4. Additional extended famiy responsibilities and commitments.
5. Increased economic responsibility over the maintenance of the double marriages.
6. Less private life for the man, since his domestic duties have increased.
7. Increased sexual demand.
8. Higher administrative ability, and common sense is called for in compromising the two families.
9. More of the husband's attention is expected by his friends, relatives and public as a whole, since, in many quarters, polygamy is seen as a status symbol.
10. There was one wife to watch over the 'discipline' of the husband, but now there are two to criticize him; that is, now he is under more social pressure to exercise his self-discipline.

It would be good to expound these points in order to offer clear guidelines

Additional accommodation

Nearly in every ethnic group, traditional polygamy requires that each new wife should have, or should eventually have her own house, *shamba* for growing her crops, granary, and livestock. It is not difficult to understand why this arrangement is an important appendix. Each wife has her own private life of course and as such, she naturally wants to have her own bedroom, kitchen, and a place she can be on her own when such need arises. Nothing seems to disturb a wife more than having her kitchen and bedroom interfered with by another woman.

But to have her own home does not merely mean having a separate house from that of the co-wife. She is allowed to have a home with her own property. 'My own thing' is the most precious feeling in life. 'My own child', 'my own bed','my own clothes', 'my own lover', 'my own God!' Traditional polygamy has done its very best to give maximum consideration to this basic psychological requirement.

We can live for another thousand years, yet any wife in a polygamous union and even in the monogamous one, would still want to have her own home and property and children. The modern polygamy is fast developing a new brand of polygamists who, unaware of this principle of successful polygamy, are treating their wives more or less like domestic animals destined to live in a common shed. These are husbands who do not seem to know why the wives of one husband cannot live (and for ever) under one roof!

A man who thinks that all he needs is a big house with many bedrooms for his wives, is committing a terrible social evil of not registering the fact that the union of a man and woman is a very personal one and psychologically it demands to be consummated privately.

Every wife has personal matters that she wants discussed within the ears of nobody else but her husband's and children's as and when it is necessary. There is a time when she wants to shut and open her own door as and when she feels like doing so. She has her personal friends and relatives whom she wants to receive privately without feeling that she is under the supervision of another woman. Only when she is accorded with such privacy can she be expected to do her best as a wife.

Naturally, she would not like to give a personal touch to a home that belongs to another wife and family. The two wives could be completely different from each other in their tastes. Although they share one man for a husband, that man should realize that the two women are not married to each other. On the contrary, he should endeavour to promote the positive sides of their differences for, after all, the marriage should be more exciting to him because it comprises two different personalities. He can force them to live in one house as the case is with some modern uncultured polygamists, but he cannot force them to like each other. When he forces them to live in one place and think alike, they, in turn, spend most of their energy consciously and unconsciously trying to fight against each other. Unfortunately, they cannot fight against each other without involving the husband and he cannot get away with it without being hurt.

If anything should set him thinking here, it should be the realization that he is, indeed, his own fighter too.

The arrangement that gives each wife her own home and property makes her feel that she has a husband to herself. Whatever goes on in the other home does not relate to her immediately and colourfully. This arrangement is also conducive to the development of better relationship between the co-wives and their children. In the old days (and even in some quarters today), and mainly because of security and communication reasons, some communities preferred having the co-wives share one protected compound where each wife had her house placed next to the other wife's. However, in many other communities where there were no security risks, the idea of keeping co-wives separated by distance enjoyed considerable support. This arrangement would be more suitable for today.

Naturally, most co-wives are rivals of each other. For the wives to live on the same compound but in different homes is not good enough, particularly in these days of material differences. Living on the same compound will make the co-wives see and assess each other daily: hence, they will get tired of each other soon. To discourage each wife from constant 'spying' of each other, each wife should live fairly away from the other; but not too far apart to make the husband's movements and communication strained.

The arrangement of giving each wife a separate accommodation is an expensive one, but so is the decision to have a second wife. Ideally, those who carry more already should not add more to their load.

There are no shortcuts to certain difficult issues of life and any effort to create a shortcut produces further complications. Noble polygamy has its stiff rules that must be kept.

Additional children

A second wife has all the rights to have her own children, as many or as little as she desires. But, especially in the modern money-times any father knows that it is not easy to manage a home with many children. Even without going into the modern economics of it, the management of children from different mothers requires more skill and dedication. In the first place, they are from different mothers who have different values; so, basically, the children of each home are different from those of the other home. Such differences can create many side-effects and constraints.

For instance, one family may produce very bright children whereas the other produces docile ones. Or some from this family may be more beautiful than those from the other family. The brighter and more beautiful ones are, of course, envied by those who are not. In some cases, this envy is capable of creating dislike. And dislike creates cruelty, sabotage and revenge. There is a much more natural agreement and tolerance among children with common mother and father, than among children who are half-brothers and half-sisters who have been fathered by one man.

Some amount of rivalry naturally exists between the two families. This can have bad results particularly if it takes the wrong course other than being a challenge to the other family to perform better. Problems emanating from such differences can be overcome only if the father has good administrative ability. This is why it is not for every Mutua and Onyango to be a successful polygamist. Again, this simply emphasizes the importance of weighing the issue of polygamy seriously before one rushes to it.

Each wife comes with her own set of problems and shortcomings to start a family. The husband must have a good sense of justice with which to handle his complex marriage. When he tries to be biased towards one family, the other family is left with no choice but to take a stance in opposition.

Increased emotional burden

There is a school of thought among many married men that marriage, although it has its good sides, is a bothersome union. For this reasons, husbands have always called their wives names. Now, this man who used to complain so much about his wife and lose his temper frequently while discussing issues with her has, finally, got himself a second wife. It is obvious by so doing, he has doubled his emotional marital burden.

In bad times he used to quarrel and fight with one wife: now he will quarrel and fight with two wives. It is the nature of married people (I think this a quality of men more than it is of women) to think or feel that they are misunderstood by the other. Now the man has got two wives to misunderstand him! And should he be one of the men who basically believe that women are nonsensical, by becoming a polygamist, he has doubled the nonsense he has to face in his home.

The biggest problem or trial crops up when each wife, as so often happens in polygamous unions, is engaged in a serious move to let the husband lose faith in the other wife. To do so, the aspiring wife may feed her husband with fantastic anti-co-wife material that includes gossip, persuasion and emotional bribes combined with any trick that is likely to make him start hating the other wife. In that endeavour, she will try her best to make the husband commit himself, 'Yes my dear, you are my number one wife.'

That automatically makes the other wife the number two. So what does being his number one wife imply?

From the moment he declares her his number one, she will start humiliating number two by saying or acting in a manner to prove the husband's thesis that, 'Since I am number one and you are number two, my priorities will be considered first.'

Of course, number two backfires, 'If it is true that I am the number two in this marriage, my husband must tell and prove to me why I am number two. Or else that woman is going to get it that she is the number two and not me'.

To effect this protest, the number two may go ahead and mobilize her friends, relatives, children and others, against the so-called number one wife. She will use her own powers and everybody she can influence to pull number one down from that status.

Where is the husband by now? How is he going to keep his hypertension low if he has one?

In some cases, though not so common, the wives formed some temporary or situational alliance against the husband in a particular issue they wanted to force through. For example, cases have been known where if the husband was getting involved with a third woman or was making an unpopular decision, the two wives ganged up against him. This was mainly because they had discovered that both were suffering from the tyranny of a man they could also fight.

If he gives this wife a present, the other wife is going to demand hers and, if possible, a better one. He himself and whatever else he has, are commodities jointly owned by the two women. It is a custom of many men to nurse the feeling that they 'own' the wives, but in practice they frequently come against odds that prove to them that they, too, are 'owned' and their movements are restricted.

Each wife tries her best always to make sure that the other wife does not get a bigger share than hers. Metaphorically speaking, they try to steal from each other if and when selfishness is at its highest. If he spends a week in the home of the senior wife, the junior wife demands to have her week with him if not more: he is a common blanket and must be shared equally when the night is cold.

When both wives are dependants of the husband financially, each wife tries to take as much of the husband's earnings as possible. When one wife has a bigger family than the other, the one with a smaller family may still insist that the husband's income be shared equally. If one wife has an income through some employment or other source while the other has not got any, she is not likely to accept the husband spending all his income on the income-less wife whom the income-wife may consider as a 'useless' wife.

Additional extended family responsibilities

Since each wife comes from a family that has relatives who look upon her for some help in one way or other (it may be a material or general help) the husband is forced to share some of that responsibility coming from the background of the two wives. Now he has two mother-in-laws and two father-in-laws with their immediate families and circles of friends. A disagreement between the two wives spills over to the 'clan' of relatives. What made traditional polygamy more successful was that, mainly, people were brought up in it, taught to accept and appreciate it; or at least, to understand or tolerate it. Problems emanating from such unions therefore, found many hands ready to help.

Double economic care

This is one thing that any man who is contemplating polygamy must consider most seriously, in particular when the marriage is going to depend on money economy. Where possible, the second wife should come only when the first wife has been settled properly.

When the man is well off, the second marriage is likely to be hastened by affluence, much more if the bride comes from an improvished background. However, as soon as the marriage takes place, she discovers that, to her dismay, the first wife is very influencial in as far as the disposition of the property is concerned and that she is not going to let that affluence or part of it, go easily to the hands of a woman who came the other day and one who has not sweated for it.

The first wife, naturally, dictates that the second wife must start from zero. There is bound to be a bitter disagreement between the two if the husband does not respect this order and simply presses ahead to make it easy for the second wife to kick off richly. It is not so much because of what the first loses in this exercise, but a matter of principle for material acquisition. A wife of a millionaire is likely to behave as crudely as the wife of a poor man would when it comes to the entry of the second wife.

The wise polygamist of these days knows the value of having material security for his big family. He knows how risky it is to base the economics of his marriages purely on salary unless otherwise his was founded upon a profession or position of great financial security. A professor may not suffer from great anxiety over what might happen if he lost his job, simply because he knows that he can still find another employment sooner or later.

If however the wise polygamist is not blessed with a secure position or profession, he can develop other resources for a second income which include finding some employment or business for his wives. Perhaps the wife who lives in the countryside intensifies her farming effort; or perhaps the one who lives with him in town engages in some form of business or office employment. A true and natural polygamist is always a busy, enterprising man.

African tradition does not encourage a wife to sit down and be fed by the husband simply because she bears him children, cooks, and keeps his home. A wife has always been a workmate, with very define duties. Western civilization has brought to Africa a lazy wife who demands support from her husband even when she does nothing else for the family except sleeping with the husband. She expects to be surrounded by servants and her food store and refrigerator should be full of butter, honey, eggs, meat, and whatever else that goes with her status. She is simply a show piece, not an active wife and mother. Everything is done for the wife in European aristocracy where everything is done for her by servants and her duty is merely to welcome guests and order servants about. This was the life of the wives of the colonialist who lived in Africa. So, the economically successful African masters who took over from the colonialists adopted the model of the white Memsahib. Today, the black Memashib sits down ready to receive nectar brought to her by servants and she expects to be served her breakfast in bed.

The practice of keeping an unworking wife seems to be preferred by husbands who want to keep the wife under their command. Since he is the provider, he is therefore her god and when she misbehaves he can bring her down to her knees by threatening to withdraw his support from her, or divorcing her altogether. She has no option but to toe his line.

It is most unfortunate for a man to add to his first marriage another dependant for a second wife who comes with these false values. It is highly recommended that the wives should be working—engaged in some kind of projects to better the economic situation and creativity of their homes. A working wife understands the value of money better than one who simply sits and waits for good things to pour in to her lap. As she gets everything effortlessly, she can afford to be extravagant. There is a saying that he who chews stones with another person's teeth does not know that it is painful.

When both wives are dependants, the degree of extravagance is great as this creates an atmosphere in which each wife tries to grab as much as she can from the husband.

The feeling nursed by some men that the husband can achieve maximum control over his wives only when the wives are economically dependant, is both a primitive and dangerous notion. In the first place such situation sets the wives against investing inspiration and, worse than that, it engages the husband in perpetual labour of running to maintain the wives solely through his own sweat. Of course, it is well-known that a working wife needs more diplomacy in handling and has more bargaining power over the husband than one without an income; but the advantages of a working wife are many. Besides, the sole aim of the marriage should not be to oppress the wife; rather it should be to liberate and help her live a life of full-realization of herself blessed with freedom. Only then can her relationship with the husband and her contribution to that marriage become meaningful.

When the two wives are working, the feeling between them that one is exploiting the husband or the marriage more than the other, and their degree of exploiting the sweat of the husband, are minimized.

However, the husband should not treat his wives as slaves and labour beasts to enrich himself and expect to get away with it. All wives look upon the husband to provide them with some amount of economic and moral support, and they naturally hate to work for the husband.

The husband can only expect the worst if he tries to force one wife to see the sense in supporting her co-wife financially. Whichever way one looks at it, the polygamist has no escape from the reality that he must work hard to keep his wives.

If one wife has an income while the other one has not, the husband should not expect the one with an income to support herself while his income goes to support the wife without. It is not the fault of the one with income that the other has not got hers. She is likely to demand an answer as to why she should be involved in the miseries of the co-wife, unless that co-wife was lame.

Employment, whatever form, has a therapeutic value. The polygamist will get less headaches from his wives if they are engaged in some kind of employment. Employment occupies their idle time which would otherwise be spent in developing or spreading bad gossip. Even when the husband has enough money to keep his wives, he should realise that he cannot satisfy them 'culturally' and that he does not have enough in terms of mental resources to keep them busy with themselves always. They need to live their private lives with other people. So far, the most modern, most productive and satisfying way known for spending one's idle time is working. A hobby such as reading is not enough; neither is it enough to be with children always. Wives and mothers get tired of being at home, with children, and alone. They need company just as much as men do. This kind of company can be found in a job or business in which the wives interact with other people and friends.

Less private time

The man has taken another woman with whom to spend his time which he had been spending with the first wife. That is, from now onwards, both wives will share his time. The day will always remain 24 hours even to the man with a thousand wives.

Responsibilities have certainly increased. Each wife expects full marital relations with him which connotes time. From now, he will be working under time pressure. Each wife is a big consumer of his time and there is bound to be a problem when one wife takes the other's time.

There is also another possible unpleasant development in that the wife who gets little time with her husband is likely to seek company outside her marriage. To achieve success, the husband must plan or budget his time properly and wisely. Even though he may not love the two equally, his time must be shared equally between them. Furthermore, it is not only his wives who need his time: his children and the other members of the family want to be with him too. This duty can be overlooked only at the expense of the marriage. Time, being the most precious commodity he has for a sound keeping of the marriage, must be shared with a high degree of fairness just like any other property the husband has.

Urban migration has created a very big problem for the polygamist whose lonely city life has driven him into a second and, quite frequently, unplanned marriage. Such marriages take place usually without the knowledge of the first wife who probably lives in the countryside. The marriages may start from a prolonged concubinage in the men's trial to solve a problem they thought was just passing.

Time distribution between the wives who are thus separated becomes a big problem. Obviously, the country wife gets the least of his time. He sees her once in a while, either when the schools close and she comes over to the city; or when he travels to see her as time and finances are available, usually at the end of the month (unless the first wife does not live far from the city). As a result, the city wife has most of the husband to herself. Perhaps she has a regular job that forces her to live permanently with him.

It would be under-estimating the issue to advise the man (as colonial missionaries did) to divorce his country wife in favour of the city one, or get rid of the city one in favour of the country one and simply live a monogamous life by bringing his wife to the place of work in order to stop the temptation of getting involved with a second woman. That actually may not be the problem. Even though he has found another favourable woman for a wife, that does not necessarily mean he does not love his country wife. The country wife may be his backbone and, in the first place, she lives in and takes care of his main home.

Many Africans still regard the city home as a temporary one. When they talk of 'home' they mean the countryside home. When they retire, they go to live in the countryside on their piece of land or farm where they will pay no water and electricity bills. It is only a small proportion of the population that can afford to own a city home. So, the city worker is a new-comer and a guest in the city. Again, due to the fact that most African cities and towns are extremely vulnerable to political instabilities which plague Africa today, most people feel that the countryside is still the castle; hence, they should spend whatever income they get in setting up a decent and permanent rural home. This trend offers the rural life a psychological wellbeing and stability.

In her protest against the city wife, the rural wife demands from the husband, 'Why do you have more time for that wife than for me—is it because you love her more than you love me?' In taking this position, however, she misses the point. For the man, the problem is deeper than the question of sex and love.

On the other hand, to the disadvantage of the first wife, the town wife, has come to occupy the accommodation that was always reserved for the first wife when she paid him a visit. In other words, the second wife has taken over the first wife's town bedroom and kitchen—a very big mistake! The first wife has every reason to feel abused.

Sometimes the husband may try to justify this position by telling the country wife that she has her own home in the countryside which should satisfy her. However, he too misses the major point that his city residence should actually belong to both wives because that is where he spends most of his working life. If it should belong to the city wife then, obviously, the city wife has not only most of the husband's time, but also a better control of his income and access to most of his friends. The situation would be worse if his income was small. In which case, the rural wife receives the least of his income as the city wife has the opportunity to 'grab' it warm from the pay envelope. In order to correct this anomaly, the rural wife may strongly feel that both wives should live in the countryside and leave the city residence free for both.

But if the husband were to agree to this kind of arrangement, the first wife is likely to put up another demand that, actually, the rural home is hers personally, so the husband should, where possible, buy his second wife her own land upon which he should build her a home of her own.

All this is mainly an economic problem which can be solved only by better income, or by affluent polygamists who have excellent means of communication, either because they have cars and can be reached easily by phone or visited any time necessary because the transport money is there. But even for the affluent polygamists, to really succeed, the rural home must not be far from the city; it must be near enough for frequent visits and checks. When the country home is far, the problem is quite acute and can be solved only by a move that bridges the distance between the two homes.

However, although in theory the urban wife has more advantages over the country wife, the country wife enjoys a more stable position. To start with, unlike the city wife, the rural wife enjoys the full moral support and sympathy of the husband's extended family and, if such family is a strong one, she can, indeed, be immovable and command a lot of power over the finance of the husband. She has a secure home (assuming that the husband has already built her a permanent home).

Modern living and situations being what they are, the city wife realizes that she sits on the weaker branch of the marriage as she has no material security like the first wife. What would happen if, she worries, the husband changed or lost his job? Or where will she live when he retires from his employment? Will the first wife accept to share her property with another woman?

For that reason the urban wife will put up a fight for her own security. She will press hard to have her own home in the countryside too; that is if he cannot buy her one in the city should she be a city-oriented person as the case is for many second wives.

Cases have been many where, finally, it was the first wife who won the battle when the economic belt had to be tightest. In which case, the man gave up polygamy and returned to the only answer—monogamy.

This economic fight is minimized if the husband can afford two permanent homes for the wives, one in town and the other one in the countryside. What then remains to be solved is the distribution of his time and effective communication. Polygamists who can afford this arrangement of homes are in a much healthier situation to enjoy modern polygamy. In which case, the two homes even become complimentary to each other since both settings—the urban and the rural—have their individual special features.

This rural urban polygamy is a modern occurrence caused by a number of factors that are not difficult to understand. The major agent of this, of course, is city employment. Today, a good number of the modern woman has access to material things through employment. Not all wives, therefore, are financially dependant on the husbands. Some of them have just as much as if not more money than the husband has. So, the decision regarding where to settle and what home to have may be influenced or even dictated by the economic might of the wife with the income. The question of financial insecurity does not enter the debate then. However, economically strong wives are not new persons in Africa and in polygamous unions.

A typical rural-urban polygamy, for example, may be created by a situation like this: The husband is a monogamist in the country side, a teacher of a low grade, married to a teacher wife. However, he is disatisfied with his profession. Besides, he is one of the ambitious young men of today. To improve on his lot, he engages himself in private study and eventually manages to do well. He passes the required exams and finally lands in a local or overseas university where he continues to perform his best. In the end he returns home as a learned man, as an academic or some professional of distinction. As things stand, or as he sees himself, he is a cosmopolitan intellectual. Unfortunately, his wife is still where she was—a primary school teacher—and even with less and less time for self-improvement because she has a big family already.

Back from college, the man gets himself a good job in the city. It is not possible to immediately transfer his family from the country to the city. Or there would be many complications if he had to effect such transfer. Perhaps because the city accommodation is too small for his family members who are much better accommodated in the countryside. Perhaps the wife has also to look after his ageing parents who cannot come to live with them in the city. Furthermore, the children are going to school in the countryside and it is not easy to secure transfers for them. If she came to the city, she might have to give up her job to concentrate on taking care of her family. Besides her teaching job, probably the wife has been keeping the farm and is engaged in an interesting project that they cannot afford to abandon.

Over the duration of the husband's studies, he evolved different values. For instance, now he may feel that he would be better off with a wife who matches his intellectual capacity; one who is not, as they like putting it, an intellectual infant. He and his first wife no longer see most things in the same persepective although they still love and understand each other. Eventually, he meets a girl who fits squarely into his pattern of thinking and values and the two get deeply involved and finally marry in his attempt to solve his kind of problem.

The new marriage creates an immediate problem for the first wife who feels very much threatened by this 'modern terrible' wife who seems to know too much with which to blind the husband from seeing his first wife. (Cases are many where such husbands returned from overseas with a foreign wife). Of course, he is happy with his modern wife, but surely, for what his first wife has been to him in the past and all the many things and experiences they shared together in those early days, not to mention the children they have raised together, he sees no way whatsoever in which he could afford a divorce. In other words, that first wife of his is so much part and parcel of him that, without her, he cannot fully appreciate the present life. Yes, intellectually they are different, but that does not and should not change the fact that she is his wife and the mother of his children.

That is that.

In the life of an ambitious and eventful man, he collects things. His second or third wife is one of those valuable collections, not necessarily more valuable than the first one. The first marriage must continue therefore, but in different gears.

Increased sexual demand

When an inquisitive Westerner meets an African polygamist, the immediate question that comes to his mind is, 'How do you go about satisfying your wives?'

Although the question has a broad implication, it is usually a sexual one. It becomes even more of a curious question when the polygamist has not only two wives but more.

It is not within the ambit of every man to sexually satisfy more than one wife; but we have emphasized elsewhere that some men are more sexually potent than others. The question is a tricky one therefore because there are no instruments for measuring potence to give the required results in answering such questions.

When the sexual part of the marriage has not been satisfied, all kinds of problems begin to plague the marriage. The monogamist who is contemplating a second wife should be sure of his sexual capacity before he embarks upon bringing another wife home. It is good if he has an idea of the degree of sexual requirements of the girl in mind. But there is a great catch here: he may never know her requirements for sure because, usually, sexual capacity is not always stable—it fluctuates between high and low depending upon the psychological charge and discharge of the person. Many men going for a second wife take for granted that they are capable of statisfying more than one wife sexually. They are not right always.

The belief that they can satisfy more than one wife is primarily based on the little knowledge they have about the sexual requirements of a woman. Most men are of course capable of having sexual relations more frequently than women due to the sexual differences between men and women. But it is actually debatable whether men are more sexed than women. All the same, what is obvious is that it is easier to satisfy a man sexually than it is to satisfy a woman and this merely addresses itself to their biological differences.

The sexual requirements of a man are mainly external, easily detected and satisfied. He can achieve sexual satisfaction with less 'details' than a woman would require to meet her satisfaction. His is more or less a masturbatory expression than an indication of love. In other words, a man does not necessarily have to be in love with a woman in order to have his sexual climax. That may explain why some men can have their climax in a rape if when they are not pathological cases. For many men if not all, any woman can satisfy their sexual desire, a wife in almost whatever mood, or a prostitute. His basic sexual requirement is that, mostly, he is looking for an 'object' with which or within which to get rid of his sexual tension. In days of great want, many resort to masturbation to rid themselves of the sexual hypertension. However, that should not and does not cheapen man's profound sexual requirements for a woman.

The physical requirements can be satisfied easily, but he has a deeper spiritual requirement which can only be satisfied by a woman of his taste and appreciation. Being in bed with a woman of high status, gives him a more rewarding spiritual life than what he would get from sleeping with a prostitute. Or when he has had sexual relations with his wife he trusts, he obtains from her both physical and spiritual satisfaction.

The sexual requirements of a woman on the other hand are more complex. The fact that biologically she is capable of performing a sexual act any time, must not be confused with her satisfaction. A man, though easily provoked sexually, cannot have sexual relations at any time because his is a physical exercise. If he does not erect that is the end of the story however much he may wish to have the relation. In order to erect, he must be sexually potent. But for a woman this is quite different because she can physically receive a man sexually at any time with or without her sexual desire, simply because there is no physical obstraction in the exercise. But to be satisfied, she needs to be in a sexual mood and that mood must be exploited to its very highest. Yet for her to be in a sexual mood, a number of other outside factors must be favourable. For example, she has to like the man in order to be sexually stimulated and she has to be in a conducive situation or environment in which her feelings are free and only then could she be aroused. Her satisfaction is accompanied by courtship in which she is made to feel that she is appreciated.

A man experiences his sexual climax with the ejaculation and in nearly all normal cases of sexual act, a man has sexual ejaculation. For a woman, it is different. Her climax comes only as the result of both physical and psychological stimulation both of which are subject to her mood. A woman needs time to warm up; a man hardly needs any time and his is a business which can be accomplished within a moment.

It is this complexity of woman's sexual requirements that the husband must be prepared to spend more time with her if he must leave her satisfied. Many men are not blessed with the kind of patience that a woman needs in order to be led to her satisfaction. To start with, not many men are capable of delaying their ejaculation once they have secured entry. So, they normally leave the woman half-way warmed up and far yet from her climax. Only when he has acquired control over his ejaculation and the skill it requires to stimulate her successfuly that the act can leave her satisfied. Sexual performance for a man depends entirely on the pre-ejaculation duration.

As seen from the above brief description, it becomes much more difficult sexually for a man to serve two wives satisfactorily, since serving one is quite demanding.

The second wife usually comes to the marriage fairly late in the man's life and, if a girl, the age gap between the two is pretty big. This is because circumstances that lead a man to decide on polygamy, are related to the first marriage and they naturally, take time to form fully. The husband may be middle aged already or even above middle age. A crisis arises when the marriage is between a girl and a man of advanced age in which he can hardly satisfy her sexually; worse still if his first wife is still sexually very active.

There are women who become more sexually aggressive after their menopause or around their late 30s and 40s. With this increased demand, the polygamist with a young wife has a big sexual task to perform. A classical example of sexual problems caused by the second wife comes when the husband realizes that, indeed, he is very much spent and cannot meet the peak demands of this younger wife who has now no other alternative but to seek satisfaction outside the marriage. In this case, the husband develops strong fears for the stability of his marriage with her. He is, obviously, afraid of losing her to those dynamic younger men. Under this situation many husbands become obsessed with jealousy and spend most of their time worrying and guarding the young wife from such men. In turn, this creates another time factor problem and the young wife's irritation over her sexual disatisfaction.

Usually when this problem arises, the first wife takes advantage of the situation and starts undermining the young wife by reporting to her husband about 'the dubious movements of your young wild wife.' So, the second wife finds herself in another problem—that of being watched and gossipped about too much. This problem could have been prevented if the husband had gone for a second wife who was not so young.

A sensible man will go for a second wife only when he is sure to satisfy her emotional needs. His big money, if he is wealthy, can do very little to help the situation to tune down her sexual requirements to match his. It is very dangerous to go for the young girl simply because of her youthful features. Such features are very expensive to maintain emotionally, financially and morally too.

If the man already has big children, it is embarrassing for them to see their father commuting with a 'child' or a girl who could as well be his daughter. The children are likely to be sympathetic with his choice if he brings home a mature woman whom they can call 'mother' without embarrassment. Unfortunately, such mature girls or women are not easy to come by, and when they exist, they are often divorcees, widows, or persons of bad or rejected character

There must be a lot in material form at the disposal of the young wife with which to tie her down to an elderly polygamist. If she is married to a big government chief who wields both economic and political power which she enjoys, or if she engaged in a business or project that she really loves, she is likely to let this make up for the other disappointment and probably look for a 'quiet' way of solving her sexual problem. As the proverb goes, one does not mind the dung of a productive cow.

The coming of a young second wife does not only mean additional sexual requirements at the highest level, but a great deal of emotional attention too. She comes, like all young women, with many illusions and great ambition, thinking that she is going to change mountains. She gets frustrated easily and starts kicking, sometimes, violently and the husband has to bear the cost of domesticating her. It is also during her attempt to solve these adjustment problems that she can so easily find herself in the hands of other men who are out to take advantage of her sexually.

In many African societies, the unfaithfulness of wives of polygynous men is not such big news. When a man has not only two but many wives, he knows that he cannot satisfy their sexual needs. Polygynous men who are emotionally mature do, somewhat, try to tolerate some obvious cases of unfaithfulness particularly if they are based on a crisis. For example, what would a man with 10 or 20 or even 30 wives do with them if not simply to overlook their infidelity?

In the case of an elderly man with a second young wife who is sexually dynamic, there is very little else he can do to keep her except to treat her infidelity with a degree of tolerance however painful it may be. Being obsessed does not solve anything. It is much better to face the bare facts. After all, the idea of marriage should be to provide fully for her needs. A lot of common sense is required to go about this problem and the least thing wanted is selfishness; otherwise, it is so easy for a second marriage to collapse under these pressures. For sure, polygamy asks for great maturity and generosity of not only material things but of thought too.

The commonest gossip among young second wives is that 'My husband becomes absolutely spent with the first "shot" when I still need several "shots" to die.'

Some Christian fanatics who oppose polygamy advance the claim that it does nothing else but promote adultery because the dissatisfied wife looks for satisfaction outside her marriage. Isn't this cheap argument: if she stays unmarried because she does not want to marry a polygamist, would she, to use the same term, adulterate less or more? Again, it is not true that if she didn't give in to a polygamous marriage, she would eventually get a monogamous husband. There are many unmarried women already in the field to warn her against such expectations.

The argument based on adultery also carries disturbing selfish views that elevate individualism above society. Is it not true that the problem of a society is a composition of the problems of individuals? Is it not true that individual efforts that encourage the society to be stable go a long way towards solving the problem of the society too?

Advanced administrative ability

There are some centres that specialize in marriage counselling. But this counselling is aimed at the monogamist strictly. This is because such institutions are based on the western values where polygamy is not considered at all.

Why are there no such African centres for handling the marital problems of polygamists? When a polygamist has a marital problem which could be cured by some counselling, where should he go? Where should the child from a polygamous family take his psychatric problems that relate to polygamy? The church which otherwise would be helpful in this course tries its best to keep away from the issue because the western theologian has taught her that polygamy is evil. The polygamist therefore, has no place in the world of psychiatric treatment.

Traditional Africa had adequate advisory provision for polygamous families, not to mention that communication between and among polygamists was easy and automatic. Wives of polygamous men lived freely and without any stigma among one another and counselled one another. In order to put up a nice face that is acceptable to modernity, majority of the 'other' wives are being treated with stigma and are therefore pushed to stay in the background where they should be seen but not heard. The western educated marriage psychologist is at a loss when he is faced with their problem.

Actually, the problems of a polygamist are more or less those of a traffic controller: to know when and when not to let such movement take place in order to avoid accidents. It is said of the first wife that she is a matter of necessity. But the second one is a matter of convenience which, of course, is maintained at a price. I think in this context it could be said of the third or fourth wife that she is a matter of luxury.

When the husband is a monogamist, he is the head or tries to be the head of one family. When he becomes a polygamist, he is expected to head the two families. Generally speaking, he should need two heads to give guide to two other heads—his wives—when such a need arises. His immediate duty and endeavour is to make the two families live and regard each other as brothers, sisters, and parents.

Could he effect this unity if he was disunited in his own actions? The answer is obviously in the negative. The old saying goes that he who can rule himself can rule the world. This saying sets off the rule for successful polygamy. That is, it is the husband's self-discipline not only in administering good conduct between his wives and children, but also in maintaining a respectable image of himself as the first and shining example that promote successful polygamy. Actually, a polygamist is not a mere husband of several wives as such, but a leader. Traditionally, it has always been the man's distinguished exercise of family leadership that eventually won him the confidence of the public to take him as their leader too. Let us expand this further by saying that he who can lead his own family successfully can lead the community. You can also say that you will know the kind of husband a man is through his own public performance. Ideally, a man's home gives him the base to practise his qualities of leadership: it is here where his administrative ability is tried best by, at least, two wives.

A man with poor organizational ability should do his best to keep to his one wife. If he cannot be successful in handling one wife, how can he be so with two or more wives? The word 'handle' is not the right one in marital matters. 'Live harmoniously with' should be the right expression. The ideal polygamist is the man who does not oppress his wives by exploiting any of his natural powers. Such is a moral polygamist. He cannot be a successful polygamist because he is a fierce wife beater, but simply because he is, indeed, a likeable person. No amount of fighting could be better than an objective guide which is, essentially, the quality of a successful polygamist. This argument seems to put forth the hypothesis that successful polygamists are born rather than made. However, there is always a great deal that a person can learn through training because a lot of the human problems as we know them, need some basic knowledge and common sense to solve and one can acquire that basic knowledge by learning.

The husband may have everything in term of organizational power, money, sex potence and what-have-you, yet he may fail as a polygamist, for example, if he was ill-equipped with the knowledge of the natural requirements of a married woman.

Public expectation

Having a second or third wife is a marital challenge that, naturally, attracts many public critics from among friends, relatives and neighbours. There is nothing unusual about having one wife—every Tom and Dicken has one; but certainly, it is something special when man takes two women under his male wings: many people become curious about such union.

The story about polygamy is not a happy one always however: many such marriages fail, and even lead the families into moral collapse. African communities live in such tight clossness that everybody's boil seems to become the concern and talk of the whole community. For this reason, there is also a lot of pressure coming from outside. When a small mistake crops up in the marriage, it is taken up by the neighbourhood and blown up into a big issue which is then fed back to the union.

Young girls want to know from the wives of polygamists what it feels like to be a co-wife; and young men want to know whether or not polygamy is something they could go for. So, they usually go about this in various ways, one of which is to raise controversial questions and debates on polygamy with regard to what they consider are the demerits and merits of such union. They are quick to criticise and pass judgement, but merely to hear what defence is given.

Obviously, a lot more is expected of the polygamist by everybody, and in order to maintain a positive image, he must keep his self-discipline belt always tight. He is also indirectly teaching his children practically all that there is about polygamy and helps them evaluate and formulate the right decision regarding whether they themselves should later enter into polygamy or not.

Wives' control of the husband

Let us say there was one wife to watch over the discipline of the husband; by bringing in another wife, he has doubled the criticism directed to him. To satisfy the two, or to live up to their expecations, he must therefore exercise more self-discipline.

Men who detest being controlled or ruled by their wives can only worsen their stand by becoming polygamists. There is a Kamba saying that a man of two wives starves to death in a place between the two homes of his wives. That is, he comes home hungry to one home but the wife in this home sends him to the other wife by saying, 'Go and be fed by your wife.' He goes to the other wife only to be told, 'There's no food here, we cooked so little and ate it up.' Perhaps she talks to him harshly and he decides to leave her alone then returns to the other wife whom he thinks would be more loving, only to find her in a worse mood. No, he says, I must go back. Somewhere on the way back he is overcome by hunger and dies. This is only a parable to illustrate some of the predicaments of a polygamist.

It is easy for the wives to relax and take things for granted. Each wife tries to push her duty to the husband, to the other wife, sometimes in protest against what she sees as her husband's more favourable treatment of the other wife.

A standing rule of any polygamist is that when he is with this wife, she should assume full responsibility as though the other wife did not exist. Under the circumstances, she cannot afford to say, 'Why don't you just go to your other wife?' He would consider such as an indication of irresponsibility and insult, unless she said so under health pressures.

In traditional Africa, it was not usual for men to share the living room with his wife. The house was considered as the place for the wife and her female children, and there was a place outside that house, open or enclosed, where the man and the male children spent the evening. As a rule, each wife was supposed to bring food to the male place where also the male guests came. No wife was exempted from bringing in her share merely because the other wife or wives had brought enough food or cooked a better meal. It was not so much the meal that was at stake, but the display of a sense of duty and solidarity.

As soon as the wives have discovered that the husband can dance to their tune at any time they wish, they can become quite unmanagable and finally push him out of his throne. Naturally, the wife's or wives' feeling is that it is much better if they can control the husband instead of being controlled by him; but the husband acts against this. The result is, of course, a struggle for leadership between man and woman.

When there are two wives or more, that struggle is more real and dramatic. This struggle may not necessarily be between the husband on one side and the wives jointly on the other side. In fact, the wives may not even be on talking terms with each other. As a result, it is a kind of struggle in which the three are pulling things towards different directions. Each wife also tries as hard as possible to assert herself, her own position, in the fear that leaving a poor administrator of a husband in the controlling position may lead to a coup or regent rule by the other wife. There is nothing more detested and unpractical than a polygamous home run by a woman in the presence of a husband. It is likely to lead the family into chaos. This does not necessarily mean that women have no leadership ability, but rather that, in this situation the challenge to the individual's survival appears so real that it provokes emotionalism which forces her to act that way. Over and above human nature is that people do not always do wrong because they are unaware of the dangers involved; they do so out of other complex reasons and forces. For example, a smoker knows too well the health dangers he is facing with smoking, yet that does not stop him from smoking. One cartoon presented a discussion between a smoker and a non-smoker in which the non-smoker challenged the smoker, 'I say, why have you decided to kill yourself slowly with smoking?' The smoker's reply was, 'Actually, I am not in a hurry to die.'

CHAPTER NINE

Accepting polygamous status

Many African institutions heavily influenced by the western cultural values have a tendency to keep silent about the question of polygamy when it is raised. Even the marital law in many African countires today sits on the fence between monogamy and polygamy. In Kenya, for example, and at the time of writing this book, the authorized form of marriage is monogamy, and the law goes ahead to say that one commits bigamy, which is punishable by law, by marrying a second wife. Yet, within that book of law, there is a curious statement that puports to cater for polygamy. It says that on the wedding day the man should declare that his marriage is potentially polygamous. That is, he should say something to the effect that, 'Though I take you today to be my lawfully wedded wife, do know that I intend to become a polygamist one time; hence, from now on, you should regard yourself as a potential co-wife until death do us part.' If not thus declared, the marrying man is bound by the law of monogamy.

In devil's name, how could you know in advance whether or not you will be a polygamist given all the facts that encourage polygamy in Africa? Obviously, this is a colonial interpretation of polygamy which is, in itself, a clear misunderstanding of African marital values and culture. It was a clause inserted in the law book therefore to frustrate polygamy. Endowed with no foresight, any marrying man is certainly unlikely to declare anything else but monogamy and by so doing he has handcuffed himself.

Yet, a substantial number of the Kenya government chiefs who range from cabinet ministers to the ordinary civil servants are polygamists. No wonder that many citizens prefer the traditional marriage to the western-styled one.

In Kenya, two types of marriage are recognized as legal. One is the marriage that has been performed traditionally, usually giving no paper certificate to the married couple and the other is the one performed in the church and through the office of the District Commissioner, both of which do issue paper certificates. A loose kind of clause exists, interestingly, between the traditional and the modern marital law: a person with a marriage certificate can securely have a second marriage performed traditionally and, within that corridor, he can marry as many wives as he wishes!

This certificate-and-non-certificate business in Kenya is notorious in bringing a lot of controversy and problems related to inheritance and other family rights. The wife holding the marriage certificate feels that she is, actually, the legal wife and owner of the man's business and body dead or alive, but not any other woman mentioned in connection with him. It looks as if the law is trying to knock the heads of the two or more wives together and tell the children of each home to hate those of the other.

The law binding one to monogamy was inserted also to conform with the philosophy of the western church, obviously in the absence of free-thinking African theologians who would have dismissed such a move as totally unchristian.

To appear in keeping with the western civilization, the African polygamist of today wears two hats. One in which he appears in the 'civilized' world—in London, New York, Paris, Bonn, Milan and so on towing and kissing only one wife. The other hat in which he appears in his village as a noble chief with more than one wife. He also chooses what word to say where and when. Quite a good number of the African presidents are known to have more than one wife, but the journalist or broadcaster who publishes anything about the other wife or wives is victimized and may even be jailed by the 'government'. This is because he has embarrassed the big man in the civilized world.

It is usually the good-looking wife, most likely the youngest who appears with the dignitary in the civilized world. The other wife, often described as 'shapeless', is kept in the background. Usually she does not speak English or French or Portugese fluently (she may not know it altogether) and she does not wear sun-shades and drink wine like the favoured wife. So, she has a good reason to envy and hate the favoured one.

However, if the 'shapeless' one wields a lot of power over the husband, as does happen frequently, and therefore would riot seriously if the husband continued to favour the 'shapely' one, the husband lets sleeping dogs lie and begins to appear in public places as 'wifeless'. This is a very curious property and practice for which the modern hypocrite

African polygamist is notorious.

Hardly any African polygamist can stand with honesty today before a whiteman and with confidence declare, 'Meet my other wife, I am a polygamist.' It is because he knows that, naturally, the whiteman is ever-ready to devaluate him if he distinguished himself as a polygamist. It is also a practice among the 'civilized' Africans not to declare such marital status among other Africans for fear of being looked down upon.

The irony is that in many parts of Africa, while there is a tendency to despise polygamy in public (or is it hypocrisy?), it is a deeply appreciated practice.

Only immaturity can make a person deny something which he really believes in. The African polygamist should, therefore, grow up and out of this shame then begin to display pride in his choice. To ignore this is not only to be dishonest to onself but also to abuse African aesthetics. He should take pride in his wives and, in a way, feel special (is he not special to be accepted by two women?) then give room for his wives to display equal pride in him as their husband. This frame of mind makes it possible for the husband to give fair treatment to each wife and display a sense of maturity not only to his children but to the public and nation as a whole.

Women married to one man should not be made to suffer or feel that theirs is not a proper marriage. The woman married to a monogamist is not, in any way, holier, better, wiser or more beautiful than the one involved in polygamy. Situations, many of which are natural, determine who gets what husband.

It is the work of the State to formulate clear regulations and laws governing the running and rights of polygamy; let the whiteman bury his own dead, but let the African bury his according to his custom.

The beginning of any worthwhile civilization is the recognition of the aspirations, beliefs, and values of its citizens. Rehabilitation of polygamy and its values is a must in Africa if we have to raise and maintain an emotionally mature and balanced nation. The town and human settlement planner, the curriculum developer and others should try their best and come up with solutions that are conducive to a polygamous community.

Should the urban centres also not have homes that are sympathetic to polygamy? African educational centres charged with training social workers and counsellors, should expand their training programme to embrace polygamy. Medical practitioners in psychiatry and psychology,

103

as well as theologians, should cater for polygamous problems. Certainly, this move would help reduce many social problems such as are created by the neglect of this aspect of our lives.

Since the decision and move to frustrate polygamy was politically motivated and implemented accordingly by colonial governments, surely, it must involve a deliberate African political decision and implementation to rehabilitate the psycho-social victims thus made.

The government should offer definite privileges to men and women entering into polygamous union, for these are the people who give substantial contribution to the government's effort in eliminating evils connected with the unmarried, widowed, and rejected women in our country.

The move to encourage polygamy should not only be implemented at the practical level, but also at the theoretical level. School education should include positive approach to the subject. Men of nobility should take the lead by stopping the hypocrisy of appearing in public with only one wife. This move should pave the right way and give moral backing to the youth and common man. What sense is there in pretending that one has only one wife when one has three? Polygamy is not a disease; like monogamy, it is a noble form of marriage.

When a polygamist is invited to a dinner party, there is no reason why he should not take his wives with him if the host so provides in his invitation. It is also absurd for the inviter to address a card to Mr and Mrs So-and-So, when that So-and-So has more than one wife. In that case, such address would be discriminatory. The African leader who is a polygamist, from the Head of State to the Headmaster of a Primary school, should free his wives and let them participate with pride in national matters. His wives deserve publicity equally. Such a move has a lot of psychological and spiritual value for the wives, the children, friends, relatives, and the national image.

It is particularly good when children of polygamous families grow up proud of their parents, with the appreciation that their parents' marital status is a noble one.

Most of the leaders of Africa today were born to polygamous parents. So, for them to rehabilitate polygamy should not be like trying to find some sense in an alien political or social theory such as Marxism. All the good literature and philosophy for rehabilitation is in Africa, produced and tested in the African workshop, developed and refined over thousands of years for the benefit of the present and future generations. Most of that literature is in oral form, which should be recorded and published.

The social sciences that govern successful marriage and co-existence as communalists, are the legacy of the present African.

CHAPTER TEN

Other Special Aspects of Polygamy

As the African traditional values that govern marriage continued to suffer big blows from the western-oriented Christian and cultural values, less and less of the aesthetics of polygamy were being heard of. So that whatever good exist in the practice today, simply remain to be the experience of the polygamist himself. Hardly anyone among the African cultural defenders has published any worthwhile work in appreciation of polygamy as an important issue of our African Experience. This omission is, however, understandable considering that most of our earlier educated Africans and educationists, academics and social scientists were themselves educated and nurtured by western scholarship; hence, they suffered from brainwashing against African cultural values. They had also to pay tribute to their 'educator' and 'civilizer' by trying, in public performances, to play down the importance of such values either by keeping silent about matters connected with the subject or slant their speech in favour of the western thought.

There was a time in Kenya (that period has not passed completely) when in a public place and particularly before any whiteman, the African could not express preference for his favourite dish. What would he (the White) think, he pondered, if he heard me saying that I prefer eating *ugali* or *githeri*, *nyoyo*, *chapati*, finger-millet stuff and so on? He felt very ashamed to admit that he ate *sukumawiki* vegetables. When he invited a whiteman, he was full of apologies for 'not-having-prepared-the-right-food'. The right food, in this case, meant chicken and rice, eggs and sausages, bacon, tomato and onion soup, steak and English potatoes, and so on.

He is still apologetic in many other ways, especially East Africans. But this is understandable again, given the period of over 60 years of political and cultural domination by the man from Europe.

In some parts of Europe they eat snails and frogs and present these as delicacy to any foreigners; but the African is ashamed to declare that he loves eating flying termites even when the story is so loud that the Chinese is not ashamed of his dog delicacy.

If Africans feel that polygamy has meaning to them, why not say so and preach so to the world? The West is also keen on learning from the African. There is a story of one American tourist who came to Africa and fell in love with the African charcoal cooked meal. He took the charcoal idea back to the States and put it immediately into commercial application. Today, in some American quarters they serve food with a charcoal 'herb' along with the salt and pepper containers to give the meal that exotic taste. When Picaso, the painter, ran bankrupt of artistic ideas and took a trip to Africa, he returned home with new inspirations from the Pygmies and his paintings took a sharp turn that made his name world famous. The Chinese cooking is highly treasured and relishly eaten the world over even though many of the westerners may not appreciate the Chinese physical beauty. There is no reason except ignorance and lack of initiative that prevent the African from exporting his culture to the internatioanal market even though the colour of his skin may be disliked by most people with a white skin.

During one of my professional tours in America, I was caught up in an argument with some Americans who asked me anxiously, 'Really how can you, or how do you go about sleeping with two wives?'

'Is it so difficult?' I treated it lightly.

'The technicalities, I mean,' one of them pursued.

In the course of the argument and exchange of jokes, one of them described in graphic details the sensation of 'group sex' in which several partners engaged in simultaneous sexual act.

'How's that possible?' I challenged him.

'Well, you see,' he wetted his lips, 'er . . . take for example, a guy having it with two girls—he's in one already while the other is watching,' he got excited, 'also doing things on the guy. As he finishes with this one, the other is dry-ready to receive him.' He let out a laughter and continued, 'Two guys can kill the girl at the same time too—one shooting through the front door while the other is shooting through the back—orchestration, I call it.'

What I found most ironical was, in spite of the eccentric sexual practice he was explaining, he found it difficult to comprehend how a polygamist goes about his sexual relations with his wives. Then I asked him something which brought him back to his senses, 'Well, how do your married men go about it with their lovers?'

"Yes, yes,' was his last answer and the argument came to an end.

Culture, every culture of the world, has many things to teach other cultures. You can say, cultures are in-laws of one another. African polygamy for example, has sensitive social values and concern for the welfare of the widow, the child, and the old. One must, of course, keep in mind that Africa is an extraordinarily big and diverse continent and polygamy takes many expressions from one community to the other. For example, among the Zulu, sororal polygamy is encouraged because it is thought to create the least friction between the co-wives who are sisters, whereas among the Tsonga there is a definite emphasis on secondary marriage with the wife's younger sister or even the wife's brother's daughter. 'If more sisters were willing to share their husband today,' argued a friend one day, 'there would be less psychopaths and prostitutes.'

Those who love each other, says an African proverb, can share anything. Professor John Mbiti, tries to defend polygamy values by saying that when a family is made up of several wives with their households, it means that in time of need there will be someone around to help.[16] This is corporate existence. For example, when one wife gives birth, there are other wives to nurse her and care for her other children during the time she is regaining her vitality. If one wife dies, there are others to take over the care of the children.

In monogamy, when the wife dies, the husband eventually brings home a stranger to the children for a step-mother who may or may not discharge the needed care. To her, these are ordinary children with no corporate relations with her. Their mother is dead, so it is their father only who knows the wish of their mother but not any other woman who has never lived with the famiy before. It has happened often that after the death of the mother, the children became totally displaced in the family with the new mother who had new and often biased leadership, so much that many of them developed into severe psychological cases. Some of them never recover from the blow throughout their life.

Traditionally, in case of sickness, other wives will fetch water from the river, cut firewood, and virtually take up all the other jobs for the family. When one of them becomes barren, others bear children for the family; when one wife is weak, other wives strengthen the family.

There is evidence that polygamy helps reduce infidelity and prostitution, especially on the part of the husband. This is certainly valuable in the case of the modern world which is plagued by so many sexual diseases and separation of married couples due to distant places of work in cities and towns, leaving their children in the countryside.

Population explosion is, indeed, a major problem of the modern nation. The high rate of birth facing the nation has grave economic and social implications in the future. The great break of polygamy and emphasis on monogamy has aggravated birth explosion. The rate of the school girl getting pregnant, for instance, is quite alarming. A big number of those pregnancies are caused by the so-called sugar-daddies during their hit-and-ran episodes. They run away from the casualties to hide in monogamy, under the Christian umbrella. One can argue that, in the case of Kenya, if the married men were sexually satisfied, less and less of them would run to the school girl. The school girl in question is trying to bear the problems of the married men who are sexually frustrated by their wives, and, of course, men who do not care for the issue of morals expected of them. When a man is sexually hungry, like anyone who has gone long without food, he tends to overlook some of these ethical huddles and proceeds to save himself with whatever is easily available and has the minimum risk. Most of the school girls in discussion live in economic dungeons and are ready to offer anything that man wants for an economic lift.

We have been making big noise with regard to punishing that sugar-daddy; however, the problem has remained how to implement that punishment he deserves, not forgetting that a big number of those offended lives in the rural areas are, in the first place, ignorant of their legal rights. In addition, too many of them would try their best to avoid embarrassment involved in trying to fight against the invincible. Furthermore, too many of those in authority, from government ministers to the school headmaster and law makers are deeply involved in the felony. In essence, the problem in question is an evil that has been socially cultivated by the modern style of living and economics.

Studies of a good number of traditional societies where polygamy has thrived show the demographer that polygamy sets the fertility rate very low and keeps it constant.[17] Co-wives are known to bear not more than one child every two and a half to three-years. This spacing is achieved by female continence and prolonged periods of lactation, a practice that inhibits ovulation. On the other hand it is a common feature among many monogamous marriages for the wife to produce a child every year.

As opposed to high fertility where the mother is crippled by frequent births, low fertility is good and highly recommended to the mother, also for the smooth running and efficiency of the marriage. Polygamy helps mothers bring their children with less stress. The importance of breast feeding has been emphasized a lot if the child has to develop mentally and emotionally balanced. This value is reinforced by prolonged lactation which is a characteristic of polygamous marriages. Psychologists maintain that much of the cohesiveness of a child's character and personality depends heavily on the child's emotional attachment to the mother, says Carothers, which is built on tactile, kinaesthetic, and auditory experience (by being fondled, rocked, carried and talked to),[18] and these are exactly what the African receives in full measure (in traditional Africa). Such individual and concentrated care can only be afforded by the mother who has good time for the child, and this good time is only available during prolonged lactation.

A good number of some of the psychological problems of the modernized African today would be reduced by the application of the principles of polygamy. Therefore, polygamy has a national importance. Institutionalized monogamy is not only oppressive to woman but discriminatory to a good number of the women in society by rendering them inferior in status. It contributes to the establishment and increase of institutionalized prostitution. From the Christian standpoint such system can be said to encourage casual concubinage and adultery since any sexual abstinence and frustration on the part of the husband which is related to the wife's period of pregnancy and lactation, is likely to drive him to the loose woman. It tempts him to engage in some temporary concubinage or forces him to seek his satisfaction from the wives of other men. This tendency has its very adverse effects too as it aggravates the chances of introducing venerial diseases and immorality into the family. A substantial part of the immorality which is found in the western civilization is manufactured by the enforcement of monogamy into the society, and the growth and survival of that immorality is catered for by the economic and educational schemes of the society.

The child of a polygamous union is born in to a richer home. A home with other children of other mothers from whom to learn quickly. His own mother is stripped off her goddess image that goes with monogamy simply becaue she is the only female person and the mother in that home. Instead, she is made a human being who is dependent upon others. The child, therefore, has other mothers besides his. There is always a great deal that he can learn from his step-mothers who make up for the weaknesses of his own mother. There is hardly any room within a polygamous home of a child to practice selfishness. Since he is born and lives among others like him, he learns as a matter of necessity, to relate to them with respect. He learns that he has to give in order to be given; to lose himself in others in order to find himself. His mother, too, learns to appreciate other mothers and children.

Polygamy is an excellent provision against loneliness—that terrible problem of the small monogamous family. In it, everybody—the father, the mother, the child, the friends—has something to do for the other. Theirs is an institution in which one is not allowed to suffer alone: his own miseries become the corpse of the corporate to put into a coffin and bury. Our first step, therefore, propounds Mwalimu Julius Nyerere, must be to re-educate ourselves; to regain our former attitude of mind; for in our traditional African society, we were individuals within a community; we took care of the community and the community took care of us.[19]

The child of the monogamist stands all the dangers of inheriting both the bad and good qualities of his parents. His world is bound to be small and his reference library of human behaviour is poor. He is brought up in an arrangement that seems to emphasize that only his own mother and father, his brothers and sisters, are all that he should love. No wonder that polygamous families have produced better, emotionally mature and successful people in public life.

The criticism levelled against polygamy, usually by the people who know little or nothing at all about it (predominatly Whites) is that it cannot be a peaceful marriage because of the jealousy among the co-wives and among the step-children. A lot of this is based upon some imaginary facts based, too, on how the western woman and man would react if they were engaged in polygamy. There is no doubt that many African women appreciate the value of polygamy in the African community. Of course, there are also African women who despise polygamy for various reasons; but this negative and positive stance is a fact of life. Even though it is accepted that marriage and having children is a good thing to the life of the human being, there are those among us too, who despise marriage and having children. But let us leave it all to the saying that one gray cat does not make all cats gray.

Of course, no human institution is free of problems. Polygamy has its problems too. It needs to be pointed out that the problems of polygamous families, says Professor Mbiti, are human problems and are not necessarily created by polygamy as such; nor have they been solved or avoided in monogamous families either in Africa or Europe or America.

The so-called jealousy among co-wives is largely a condition of the mind and depends very much upon the cultural background in which those women were brought up. A woman who grew up in a polygamous marriage would tend to appreciate polygamy more than the one who was brought up in a monogamous setting. When a European goes to Japan and sees women giving their seats to men when travelling, the immediate reaction is that the Japanese woman is oppressed and that, consequently, Japan is a man-society, and that it is needful that a woman liberation movement be registered to start fighting for woman's right. That she may be oppressed may be true, but one may also want to know how the Japanese woman views the situation. Moreover, that does not necessarily indicate that the Japanese woman is more oppressed than the European or American one.

It is when Europe and America take the throne to judge other cultures, obviously through their own cultural sieves, that these problems are amplified. The average European or American cannot imagine the fact that, from an African point of view, there are many wrongs in those countries. If an African man refuses to use a toilet that his mother-in-law has been using, it is for a noble reason; but to a European such may make no sense whatsoever.

The boundary of cultures is respected by sensible men; as the Italian would say, only when you have been eating spaghetti will you learn to appreciate it.

Polygamy, monogamy, sex, power, money, children, etc., all are subject to abuse. That is, every human institution has loopholes for exploitation. The wife of the monogamist can also suffer from obsessive jealousy; she can grow terribly sharp horns too. There are many monogamist wives who hold their husbands' sexual requirements at ransom. And there are countless monogamist husbands who cook hell against their wives merely to justify a divorce in order to get the other woman who looks better and more understanding.

The truth is that, in Africa, there are countless wives of polygamists who live a more peaceful and happier life than wives of other monogamists.

Over and above, as the relationship between man and woman is of personal nature, it is only good and wise that the decision to be a polygamist or otherwise be left to the individual man and woman when all the necessary advice has been offered to them. Let us also not forget that the single woman who takes herself to polygamy, knows her problems better than the married woman. Once, there was an argument between a mother and her daughter in which the daughter, believing strongly that her mother was misbehaving because she was seen with an 'authorized' man, took it tough on her, 'Mother, what the hell do you think you are doing with that man?' The mother's answer was quick, precise and straight, 'Keep your nose out of my affairs; you cannot have pleasure on my behalf.' There is a tendency to blame polygamy on men without saying the least common sense that it takes a man and a woman to enter into polygamy. In Africa, women are not drafted into polygamy; they participate in it fully. We are sometimes carried away by semantics: women, for example, don't create prostitution; prostituion is created and shared equally by men and women.

CHAPTER ELEVEN

Toward Successful Polygamy: Gears that Perfect Polygamy

Respecting individuality

The man begins with one wife. Then the second one comes because of whatever reasons. Two female persons come to live with him; therefore, three people are now to live, using biblical language, as *one* in a unity called marriage. Or in an industrial language, the three new form one organization in which they are all signatories.

Since it is the man who brings the two women together, generally speaking, it is taken that he is and should be the head of the two wives. The role of this *head* has always defied definitions by the nature of its complexity, and I do not see any useful need for me to try to define it. One reason is that marriage means different things to different people. However, I cannot help indulging in some generally accepted notions that contribute to a form of definition.

In traditional Africa, a home is a home when it has a wife; otherwise, it should simply stand out as a mere house. From this persepctive, the polygamist is therefore, the head of the two homes. In crude language, he may like to see himself as the boss. But family and marriage affairs argue that there are no bosses at home; bosses are in the office. The language that may come closest to the description is that, marriage is an organization or a domestic government of corporate nature; and in a corporation, frankly speaking, each partner has no absolute power.

The recognition or acceptance to operate by the rules of a corporate system is the beginning of a healthy union, be it monogamous or polygamous.

Imaginary and real

When the man is thinking of bringing another wife to his life, surely, he is visualising many positive ways of running the plural marriage. But a lot of what he thinks at this stage is theoretical. No one can really know precisely what becomes of one's marriage until one has lived that marriage.

Again, what he thinks prior to living a polygamous life is primarily based on the image of his first marriage. Unfortunately people are different and, basically, they are individuals. This, he realizes as soon as he has brought the second wife home. He finds out that some of the principles he had been employing in his life with the first wife, are totally unworkable with wife number two.

Let me finally dismiss the words 'principle' and 'organization' from the discussion of marriage and come closer to the real issue of marriage—emotion. Whatever form of marriage, the sound and successful marriage is managed more than anything else by the interplay of emotions and common sense. Marriage isn't something you've got to organize and manage, argues Mace.[21] It is a fellowship to which you have to yield yourself. We have to be careful lest we forget to live, so preoccupied with obeying the rules we have learned that we fail to respond to the deep urges within us, so self-conscious that we lose the power to act spontaneously. The trouble with the modern man is that he is, as he likes to put it, 'running his life.' That is all wrong. Life should be running him.

Healthy marriage, polygamous or monogamous, should run the husband, not the husband to run it. The exaggerated DOs and DON'Ts of the husband may easily overlook the fact that, marriage is mainly a matter of emotional interaction where each partner reacts differently to different issues.

The husband should be prepared to ask his plural marriage, 'How do you want to have it?' Instead of ordering, 'This is how we shall have it, fullstop.'

The value in the difference

After all, he married the second wife basically because he thought she was different from the first wife. It is ridiculous therefore to try to mould her to fit into the shape of the first wife.

If we accept that marriage is a partnership in which each comes to the other after realizing his or her own limitations in living alone hence the need for the other in order to live a full life, then marriage should be based primarily on the foundation of the differences between the married persons. The husband can succeed in his marriage only by looking at the wives and appreciating them as different persons.

Each wife has her own ambition. For this reason, he should help her realise her ambition in her own rhythm if such aspiration is a good one both to her and her marriage. We all do not like singing the same song although certain songs happen to be more popular than others. That is, the polygamist should encourage each wife to sing her own favourite tune. He would be making the worst mistake to take the two as mere inter-changeable women who happen to be his wives.

A man who is looking for a second or third wife to add a number to his field of command, is making a great mistake and he should not be surprised when his wives turn against him. There is a story told of a lover who made love to his girlfriend and left her very thrilled. But shortly after the love episode he made great enemies with the girl when he had a slip of tongue and called her by the name of another girlfriend 'You're a beast!' she cried. 'All that time you were making love to me, you must have been making it to that other woman in absentia—go to hell!"

No one wants to be mistaken for another. We may love to copy others by trying to look like them, but we always copy them subconsciously steal all that is good from them and put it in us. Everybody considers themselves more important than others. In other words, nobody wishes or thinks that the other person is and should be more important than himself. 'The beginning is,' says Dale Carnegie, 'I am the most important person on earth'[22]

Each of the two wives, therefore, unmistakably considers herself more important than the other. So, the husband's attempt to correct this view or make her give up this feeling, will only land himself into more problems. Rule number one for the polygamists, then, is that he should treat each wife as though she were more special than the other, and he should never make the mistake of comparing one wife to the other particularly in uncomplimentary manner, for example 'Agnes makes better tea than you.' The very immediate question that comes to her mind in response to that comparison is, 'So, does that mean that Agnes of yours is better than I?'

It may be a fact that the Agnes in question makes better tea, but it should not be put in such a way that it bruises the ego of the other wife. It should not be said in the first place; he should simply show her how to make better tea, and not suggest that Agnes should teach her how to make it. He is the one who should learn from Agnes how to make it then teach the other wife.

Avoiding gossips

The opposite should also be avoided, 'You make better tea than Agnes.' Although this statement is an ego-booster to the one told, it carries the danger of being exploited by Milka to humiliate Agnes. What if Milka goes and, during one of those many loose discussions or arguments with Agnes, discloses, 'Actually, he says that I make better tea than you.?' Agnes will not take that kindly. If a praise has to be given, it should be made in appreciation of the individual. For example, he could have said, 'I enjoy your tea very much.' That, of course, does not mean he does not enjoy Agnes's tea equally or even better. In this case, there is possibly no clever way in which Milka could exploit the statement to humiliate Agnes.

The polygamist should always desist from discussing the weaknesses of the other wife with the present one. Such discussion is likely to prepare the ground of attack during personality clashes which so often crop up between co-wives. Milka for example shall elevate herself by pushing the other to a lower status by trying to prove Agnes how much, in fact, Agnes is so unpopular with the husband because of her many faults. Even positive praises may be misunderstood and turned against the other person. Perhaps he has told Milka, 'You know, Agnes has proved herself quite intelligent lately.' Although this an apparent harmless statement, Milka is likely to take it as an attempt to draw a distinction between who can apply her mind to issues correctly and who can not. The unasked and unanswered question that comes to Milka is 'What about me—haven't I proved myself intelligent? Is she more intelligent than I?' What this means is that, by implication, his statement about the intelligence of the other woman, was of comparative nature. The statement may also be taken on the suspicious note that the husband is out to impress Agnes's intellectual aptitude on Milka.

Change of the scapegoat

It is in man's nature that when something goes wrong, he or she tends to blame it on an outside agent. When the husband had one wife, he used to put the blame of his marital dissatisfaction on the weaknesses of his one wife. So he thought he should really settle down as soon as he had married himself another woman. Finally, he brought her home; but now he has discovered that, in fact, he did not solve the problem fully. Or rather, the scapegoat has changed. He may think that Milka has adopted this unbecoming behaviour just in order to register her protest against some special favours she thinks are extended to Agnes.

In a way, one can say that the second marriage if based on the emotional dissatisfaction of the first wife, does not solve all the problems of the first marriage. But if it solves them, it does so also by inviting others of a differnt kind.

Wife-beating and use of force: The right and wrong of the issue

The factors behind wife-beating, including husband-beating, are many. One can't say off hand that wife-beating or husband-beating is wrong. A lot of this depends upon the circumstances in which these happen and the character of the person involved. So, this discussion is not out to approve or disapprove marital violence. However, and this as a matter of necessity, what must be said here is that the coming together of two women to depend on one man in one way or other or to relate to one husband, in so many ways, plays with the balance of power structure between man and wife. As was said in another chapter, there are now two persons (women) against one person (man).

It is so natural that at a complete loss of his wit, or when seemingly he is being over-powered by his wives, the husband gets tempted to use his physical superiority, to rule by force, that is. I remember some disturbing reasoning advanced by one of our teachers when he was punishing a pupil who had not grapsed his lesson properly. The teacher argued that he was not beating the pupil but the mistake when, in fact, it was so obvious that the teacher could not, physically or otherwise, beat a mistake; he could only beat the pupil and that was all. This argument is sometimes used by some husbands when they beat their wives.

Frankly speaking and according to natural law, violence has its room in every situation of life. However, one should note that, strictly, violence has and should have its place, time, and suitable measure.

In the first place, life itself is violent. We are born through a violent birth. Many situations of life, if not all, are far from being peaceful. Yet, and by natural law too, peace has its place, time and suitable measure in our lives. Perhaps the best that could be said in this context is that he who lives this life must always endeavour to strike a balance between violence and non-violence; or rather learn to put up with them the way one puts up with the thought of life and death for, otherwise, if there were no life there would be no death. That is, death, is, because life is.

Isn't it true therefore that if there was no violence, peace would not be realised? There is daylight so that there may be night. There is no 'high' if there is no 'low'; there is no 'far' if there is no 'near'. There is white so that there may be black; there is bitter so that there may be sweet. I think it is the contrast, the polarity between bad and good that makes life dramatic; therefore, sin and innocence are relative terms both of which, in a way, depend on each other and hence indispensable to each other. That does not make attractive religion, I am aware, but if it is overlooked it becomes an unfortunate omission.

The law of successful leadership, be it domestic or political, monogamous or polygamous, lies in the art of ruling; how to make the ruled not feel ruled. Or the art of giving and taking away without making the given feel that they have been given and robbed. When too much is given, that creates problems too. As the saying goes that too much of everything is poisonous.

A polygamous man knows that, once in a while, and quite often in other cases, the wave may be in favour of the wives to join forces against their husband. Women are not endowed with physical strength with which to confront man when a violent situation arises. Of course, we have seen some women on the boxing and wrestling ring and in karate exercises beating some men, but such are exceptionals. However, although women are physically inferior to men, they have, indeed, other superior powers over men. To sound a radical note, women are not as harmless as they may appear both to themselves and to men.

Psychological fight

There are two kinds of fights: the physical and psycholgical fights. It is debatable which one of them is stronger than the other. One of them, the physical, is feared more than the other, but this is mainly due to the ignorance with which the psychological one is greeted. The psychological one is abstract, its results are nebulous like a sickness in the bloodstream which you cannot feel directly but only through its results on the body as a whole.

A person can be subjected to psychological violence that is as fatal as one effected by physical violence. There are many fatal psychological diseases. Again, it is debatable whether less people suffer or die of psychological diseases than of physical causes.

Whereas man is well-known for his physical attributes and violence, woman is known for her psychological violence. As one may like to dramatize it: a man beats, but a woman bewitches. That is, in their negative attributes, a man is principally a beater and a woman a witch.

The world is divided between two forms, the 'seen' (physical) and the 'unseen' (metaphysical) forms. In other words, what is seen with the eye including that which can be felt or touched, is not at all everything about life. My hypothesis is that the seen world should balance with the unseen world.

Man's powers seem to be concentrated on the physical side whereas woman's tend to be banked on the metaphysical. Hence, both man and woman are essentially different people physically and emotionally. As some men have sometimes put it, the two are of different tribes.

Nature is not unwise to leave the polarized man and woman defenceless against the powers of each other. I believe that the powers of each cancels out those of the other so as to create a balance.

Psychiatrists may keep the list of how many deaths men have died by the psychological violence subjected to them by women, just as doctors can tell how many women have died through the physical violence subjected to them by men. The alcoholic seen in the bar every evening may as well be a manifestation of the psychological violent wife he has at home. What I am trying to say by all this is that when a wife is beaten or when she is provoked, she has her own way of fighting back and her retaliation may not necesarily be milder than the husband's blow. He becomes even more vulnerable if he has to fight with two wives.

The kind of psychological torture that a woman exerts on a man is immense. In Mao Tsetung's language, as the husband sharpens the sword of his physical power, his wife sharpens hers too. The winner is not, so often, the husband as frequently expected.

Violence as a means of solving marital problems should be kept strictly at its natural level. Violence does not build a home, goes an African proverb. It is always much better to go back to the corporate approach. Accepted that it is impossible for people who live together to avoid some form of friction as the proverb puts it that axes in the same basket cannot avoid tinkling—but much of that friction between the husband and his wives could always be reduced by trying to avoid positions and matters that create more or aggravate friction.

Although the practical side of life tends to justify the position that a foolish question deserves a foolish answer or that a bad deed deserves punishment, frequently it does pay to take a philosophical view by taking into consideration other dynamics that could have influenced the course of action. A philosophical consideration shows that it is not true always that a bad deed deserves punishment.

One can still try to stop the axes from too much tinkling by putting some cushion between them. In marital terms, this cushion is common sense, justice and forgiveness.

The problem of woman

Freud said that the problem of a woman is that she does not seem to know what she wants. Yet her basic expectation and desire is that she should be understood. One man reacted to this contradiction by snapping, 'How on earth do you try to understand a woman when she does not know what she wants, yet she behaves as though she knew precisely what she wants? The psychiatrist inverviewing him replied, 'What you have said is already a good beginning towards understanding woman.'

This is not meant, in any way, to mock the intelligence of woman. But neither am I out to justify the so-called intellectual equality between man and woman. Man and woman are ment to complement each other. In other words, man's intelligence needs woman's in order to gain balance. Woman's intelligence, too, needs man's in order to be complete. This is the farthest one can go with this equality issue, for nature saw that neither woman's nor man's life was complete without that of the other.

But following the natural attributes of the two further, what should not pass unsaid is that, putting it in poetic language, wheres a man 'sees' a woman 'feels.' Is it not absurd therefore to argue that 'seeing' is better than 'feeling'? Certainly, the two cannot be compared because they are the two sides of the same coin called perception. Indeed, 'seeing' and 'feeling' complement each other to achieve better perception.

'Seeing' is the basis on which physical science is primarily developed and 'feeling' is the stem on which non-science is made. 'Seeing' can be represented by 'reason' and 'feeling' can be represented by 'emotional reaction'.

When it is said that woman is emotional and man is rational (these are generalized statements of course) that statement or claim usually offends woman. This is because 'emotion' has in the past been associated with having little or no thinking aptitude at all. Yet, if one had to be rational about the whole argument, man should be offended too by being referred to as 'rational', simply because this would tend to exclude 'emotion' from his perception and as we know it, 'emotion' is a human quality that is so vital to a balanced life.

The truth is that man does not and cannot live by 'reason' alone. To be 'all-reason' would make him a terrible machine that has no feeling. But neither could he live by 'emotion' alone because again; that would make him a horrifying animal devoid of reason.

'Reason' and 'emotion' therefore, are the two sides of the same coin. Nature has distributed the two sensibly in that 'reason' is a predominant quality of man and 'emotion' a dominant quality of woman. It is only when the two are confused as it were, that each person takes the washing of the other, that a chaotic situation of living is created. The natural truth is that woman cannot become a man and a man cannot become a woman. During one symposium and in a woman liberation argument, Pamela Mboya of Kenya articulated, 'Even if man and woman became equal woman would still have to bear the children.'

The great mistake that the western civilization has made is to take 'reason' as the only basis of life, and it is this position which has developed male chauvinism since, naturally, man tends to be more gifted in 'reason' than woman. Physical science, a discipline of education that lies more in man's natural ability than in woman's has promoted man's ego unreasonably, hence pushing metaphysics down more and more as a discipline that does not make man equally progressive. Physical science, therefore, promised heaven on earth. Yet physical science confronts the human being with terrible threats today.

'Science is in decline', argues Professor David Horrobin, 'because it is obvious that it has failed to provide answers to any of the really important problems of the world. In spite of the phenomenal growth of scientific activity, if anything the problems are becoming more and more serious. What is worse, science is actually responsible for some of the most unpleasant disasters. Science will survive,' he contends further, 'only if it controls itself, only if it takes care to stress the limited areas which it is valid, only if, no matter what pressures, it refuses to go beyond its proper frontiers, only if it ceases to proclaim itself the panacea for all ills. I think that one line of research which should be stopped forthwith is that into methods whereby human parents may choose the sex of their children. The adverse effects of such choice exercised on a large scale could be socially disastrous as parents in most societies seem to prefer sons to daughters and this could lead to a gross excess of males and to all the horrors and violence of a society in which this situation occurs.'[23]

This is always the result when man tries to imbalance nature. 'Feeling' tells us something else. That something somewhere is wrong. What a child needs when he is born is not 'reason' but 'emotion', or rather, emotional care combined with reason. When the child cries, that cry gives his mother pain, so the mother attends to the child. When a relative dies, 'reasons' says that death has come and, by 'reason' we all shall die one time or another, so there is really no need to weep for a dead person, for even if we wept blood for tears to express this grief, nothing would bring the dead back to life.

All these are excellent emotionless facts, yet with all of them we are struck by the reality that something is yet wrong because we have lost a beloved person with whom we shared so many experiences of life and that,

that something called 'death' has put a full-stop to any further sharing of those good things. That is, something really big has been subtracted from our lot, so we are justified in feeling sad and weeping for the departed one.

'Reason' alone teaches us how to be bloodless, emotionless because, by reason, pain is unnecessary. Whereas the ability to feel pain is perhaps the most important of all senses. If I had to lose a sense, says Horrobin, pain is the one I should fear the loss of most.[24] Pain is vital if a young creature is to grow up normally and if an adult one is to pass through life relatively unscathed. Pain is the sensation that warns that fires are hot, that knives are sharp, that broken limbs must be rested, that medical attention must be sought. Without pain no wild thing could go beyond infancy without being cripped. Without pain even human infants with protective parents would be horribly deformed after only a few years of life.

To save man from all these terrible things, nature has put something in him or her to take care of things; something that, quite often works by instinct, warning us that something somewhere is going to happen if ... A sensitive inbuilt instrument that makes the doer suspicious or hesistant without any apparent cause. So that when 'reason' becomes combined with that inside thing, the right decision can be taken.

The fact that Man is classified as an animal and animals are known to work best by instinct, gives us a strong argument that Man cannot have been denied of this invaluable agent of self-preservation. Unfortunately, man seems to forget that many of his problems could be solved by sheer instinct. To yield to 'emotion' when necessary is, therefore, a wise move.

If then by the gift of nature, woman is a child of emotions as some people may like to put it, it should be correctly said that her world is as important as that of her counterpart, man. Furthermore, if she surely does not know what she wants according to Freud, it is because she is endowed with a very advanced capacity for feeling in which she gets entangled up so easily. Of course, how can she know what she wants always when life expects too much of her?

The struggle in the West for woman to cease being a woman and become a man is very well known and documented. But all this is due to the mistakes of placing too much emphasis on the aesthetics of man at the expense of the woman's, hence man becomes a worshipped being in the West. This is, as it were, to create too much manpower without womanpower. Don't we need just as much womanpower as we need manpower?

The Biology lesson tells us that the spark of life is caused by the union of the male and female cells on contact. Does it therefore matter what cell fertilizes the other or, as some men like to put it, who lies on top of whom in sexual relations? To enter a house, a door must open for the visitor; if it does not open, no entry can be effected. That is, it is not merely the entering that rules opening: every action is described by two parallel happenings before it can be complete.

It cannot be emphasized any further what dangers lie in the attempt to make woman man. Homosexuality does not do away with the importance of the other sex. If only the fight could stop where woman fight to be man and man tries to create a man out of a woman, the world would be a more balanced place. There would be fewer marital quarrels, fights, divorces if they would still be there at all.

For a long time, the West has been trying to make woman abuse her own role and importance and many women have responded to that brainwashing warmly. However, the bitter consequences have not been woman's alone. They have been shared by both man and woman. There was a cartoon published in one of the Kenyan dailies in which the man wore woman's clothes and said, 'Since woman can wear man's clothes, for equality, why shouldn't I wear woman's clothes?'

As for clothes, perhaps, each could wear what the other wears, but they should never try to exchange their differences, for such would be very destructive.

The problem with some married persons is that, frequently, they seem to forget why they married. The husband married his wife because she was a woman and the wife married her husband because he was a man. So why should they now engage in a struggle to convert the other into the opposite sex?

On the other hand, let this discussion not imply in any sense that there are always very clear, dividing lines between everything each sex does. There is, of course, a great deal of similarity between man and woman. Perhaps the parable of their likeness is in their physical features. If it were not for the beard and absence of breasts and muscles, it would be difficult sometimes to tell whether or not you are looking at a man in the street. There are a few but deep special features in each sex that make all the difference. But there are the physical and spiritual differences that make their relationship deep and healthy.

This long digression from the use of force and violence in marriage, was only intended to show further the basic differences between man and woman, and it is here where things should begin in the appreciation of each other's outlook on life. When these differences are understood and taken seriously and respected, there should be less problems and fights between a husband and his wife or wives.

Material differences

Quite often, polygamy brings together to one husband women of diverse differences. Hypothetically speaking, the more the two wives differ from each other, the more struggle is likely to spring up between them.

If, for example, the coming of the second wife was due to the husband's growth in intellectual aptitude leading to his second wife against his first wife who had little formal education or mental development, it may be assumed that the second wife makes up for what the first one lacks. Therefore, both marriages should be happy. But in practice this is not always the case. Or before the second marriage the husband was frequently complaining that his wife was not speaking an international language, or could not participate in intellectual discussions in important functions. So, what are his complaints now that he has got himself a well-educated wife who matches his status?

If Agnes is a university graduate and Milka is a primary school graduate who has been living with the husband for many years, by virtue of her better educational standard, Agnes is in a better position to bully Milka. But Milka is in a different priveleged position too to bully Agnes by the virtue of having lived with the husband for a longer period of time and getting children who may be already quite big and who give her husband a lot of pride. Her marriage, for this reason, has been more realised and she has got very deep roots in this man's life. She can very easily look down upon Agnes and even afford to think or say that Agnes is merely a cheap third-class wife who could not find herself a free man to marry.

That is, with their differences, each wife capitalizes on hers during any struggle, to humiliate the other. However, this struggle is minimized when there is little material difference between the two wives. The same struggle may also ensue from differences attributed to physical features when one wife is more beautiful than the other or, as in a classical situation, from one wife having a paying job while the other not having one.

Even when the first wife had participated in the decision to bring in a second one, that decision does not stipulate that friction between the two wives should never arise. It is much healtheir for the husband to start off with the expectation that, from time to time and because of one reason or another, the wives will clash with each other.

Polygamists devoid of the basic human psychology expect their co-wives to love each other. That is expecting too much really. It is more pragmatic if the husband tries to lay down the foundation for his wives to love each other, but he should not be too ambitious in this move. One of the ways of promoting that love and respect for each other is by engaging himself in any activity that encourages corporate feelings between the wives. Such may be achieved, for example, by showing how and where the two need each other and how much they could achieve by pulling things together. Unfortunately, it is not common for both wives to be equally active or industrious. One may be a terrible spendthrift while the other one frugal. One may be religious while the other one is superstitious. In a situation like this, any move on the part of the husband to encourage togetherness is likely to be defeated by the opposing qualities of both wives.

The other practical way of looking at it is that there is not much between the wives that should make them love each other, particularly because they are placed in a polarized situation. They are only likely to co-operate with each other if their differences are complementary. For instance, in a situation where the first wife is childless and the second marriage was called in by the wish to have children for the family, the first wife is likely to extend her warmth to embrace the second wife who is her redeemer. The same applies if the first wife suffers from ill-health, making it a cause for a second marriage.

She can also co-operate with the first wife warmly if the marriage had been initiated by the first wife who, for one reason or another, wields tremendous powers over the husband and is likely to cause havoc to a second wife who does not perform her functions properly. In this case, the second wife looks upon the 'Mama' as her defender. Equally too, if the first wife is loving, magnanimous, and understanding to the second wife, the second wife is likely to reciprocate warmly. But a lot of room for co-operation depends upon the degree of fairness with which their husband treats them.

However, human nature being what it is, it is not always possible for them to co-operate irrespective of the circumstances they may be in. For example, if Agnes gets the son that the husband had been longing for from Milka without success, Milka, even though she may clearly see that this so-much-desired son is also for her own marital stability and security, may be forced by her own feelings to react unfavourably, either because she is jealous, or because she feels and fears that the gold shall now stop coming to her and start flowing into the hands of the valuable Agnes.

A lot could also be said about a situation in which, as it has been noted among many such contacts, the 'blood' or vibrations of the two wives do not agree with each other in spite of the favourable position that marriage has bestowed upon them. There are people you just don't like, said one woman, although you don't know why or perhaps because you don't want to know why.

Parental care

When the wives are warring with each other, the children are forced to take sides with their mothers. The cause of the fight may, of course, also stem from the children themselves. There are simply too many things that can start the mother-to-mother or children-to-children fight which may range from spiritual, gossip, to economic reasons, from within or without the marriage.

It is natural that if Milka picks a fight with Agnes, Milka's children will sympathize with their mother even when it is apparent that Milka is wrong. They cannot simply be expected to crucify their own mother for whatever cause. In retaliation, Agnes is likely to mobilize the power of her own family against the 'enemy.' This situation puts the father in a very difficult position since he is the only bridge between the two families. Each family, naturally, expects him to take sides with them against the 'enemy'.

Usually many polygamists have a soft spot for one wife and her family which may be as the result of some historical facts. It is then so easy for such a husband to be drawn into defending the favourite family even when the mistake lies with that favourite family. But really wise polygamists have been known to always try as much as possible to take a neutral stand in matters of this form. They know that to take sides with one family can be disastrous.

Of course, he can be frank and tell Milka before Agnes, 'You are the one who is wrong.' However, he must make sure that Agnes does not, from now onwards, nurse the feeling that she is the good wife and Milka is the bad one. He should make a distinction between correcting a mistake and condenming a person.

His major responsibility towards the children of the two wives is to bring them up with a strong sense of responsibility towards each other. He should bring them up bearing the unquestionable feeling that the mother of the other step-child is just as good and helpful to him as his own mother. And that Milka's children are just as good and helpful as those of his own mother Agnes and, indeed, all of them are simply brothers and sisters of one family. For that reason, it is expected of each to be kind, helpful; forgiving to the other.

The children, just like their mothers, should not be made to feel that they are less loved than the children of the other mother. Swopping duties and other responsibilities between the families is an ideal exercise that helps cultivate unity between the families. That is, the children of Milka should take pride, or be made to see sense in carrying out duties for the family of Agnes. If Milka has a son or daughter who is gifted in one thing, his or her service should not be exclusively for her own family. He or she should be encouraged to make the other family happy with that gift because it is also possible that Agnes may one day get a child who could be very useful to the family in a different way. The important thing is to appreciate that nobody is and could be self-reliant.

This, of course, is easily said than done in real life. But it is true that where there exists room for reciprocity, better things are done and achievement attained than where unity is given less importance. This exchange of services between the children is not merely for the benefit of the parents but for the children too. Here, they are given a chance to develop a strong relationship among themselves. There have been so many cases where, in later life, it turned out that a step-sister or step-brother was more understanding and useful than a full sister or brother. As it can and has been said, the best brotherly or sisterly love is not always necessarily from one's owns brother or sister. It can come from without the family of one's own mother.

Within this large family, the single child is given a wider field from which to develop and choose his or her best family friends unlike within a monogamous family where there are only a few relatives to choose from. The good relations he is privileged to develop from the larger family will, later, form part of his personal 'asset' or 'army' in the struggle for living when his parents are too old or dead.

Regarding the group which is better prepared for family responsibilities, the family with a bigger number of children will always find it easier to carry out a given task than the small number of the monogamous marriage. Having more brothers and sisters therefore, helps the individual child bear less of the family load. However, one must admit, this is positive only as long as the economics of that family are healthy enough to cater for the many brothers and sisters; otherwise, being born among many brothers and sisters who demand economic care from meagre resources can be disastrous particularly in these days of high cost of living.

Most African states today are extremely ill-equipped with social security programmes for old age. The retirement age is, for most salaried people, the very dead-end of their economic independence. From now onwards, the old man and old woman have to be given food, clothes, medical care, etc. by their children. Hence, they have become a liability when once they were assets. As the saying goes, the herdsmen have changed hands permanently: the young have taken things over. If such a retired parent has a few children or none at all, and if such children have no good income with which to take care of their own individual families in addition to the old folks, the situation becomes extremely difficult for the old parent.

So, one side of looking at this national social issue is that, until such time as the State has developed comprehensive social security programmes for the old and the other unfortunate citizens, that security must be built on children and solid familyhood. In this context and for the sake of survival, the family should be organized to act as a dynamic training centre for the fighters. The bigger and stronger the battalion, the better chances of good living. Nothing has really changed that much since the dawn of life: man must hunt for his living, and the more he is equipped with hunting tools and company, the better his survival.

The sense of belonging to somewhere, somebody, and to something big, is man's strongest desire. It is a good feeling for the individual person to feel that 'I belong to a strong family.' If something bad happens to him, it is a good feeling to have that there are other people who can come to his moral and material help.

The criticism levelled against polygamy is that it involves a big family, and that it is difficult to bring up a large family successfully. But this is not anything big to scare the polygamist. After all, where the risks are high, the degree of gain and satisfaction is also raised. There is also another advantage the polygamist has over the monogamist: he has 'many' brains (more brain-power that is) at his disposal. A problem that would paralyse a monogamist with his small family, would probably be solved more easily by a large family because of its more diverse ways of looking at things.

With regard to brain-power, two wives are better than one at work with the husband. From this angle of argument, one can understand easily the saying that monogamy is a poor form of marriage, simply because:

   (a)   its labour force is less
   (b)   its social compound is less
   (c)   its brain-power is less
   (d)   its unity for survival is less.

It is this feeling of being more protected (by a larger family) that enrichens the child of the polygamous home and which, so often, makes him feel superior to the child of the monogamous home.

'Many' has always been better than 'few' in terms of service. The question of what is too many and too few, in this context, is culturally determined.

The price to pay

But all these good things which can occur to the large family become a reality only if the big man of the homestead is a good and hardworking husband. A good father of his children. A family man.

The noble polygamist is a kind man who is level-headed. One who is patient and vigilant and quick to act in combating the devilish side of his establishment. The polygamist is surrounded by many temptations and challenges, particularly when jealousy enters one side of his family. Or, in worse situations, when jealousy has perched on both families.

There are many cases where the jealous wife has been known to resort to excessive attempts at eliminating the 'enemy'. Witchcraft cases of one wife trying to bewitch the children of her co-wife, or bewitching the co-wife are not few in this case. However, these evils and others thrive better where both administrative ability and sound foundation of the marriage are lacking.

When the homes are separate it is easier for the children of both families to live with less friction, and that in itself enhances better relationship among them. Possible jealousy between the mothers is also minimized since there is less time to see or notice that which is likely to cause envy.

If Milka is more privileged by nature in one thing or another than Agnes, the children themselves are bound to notice that difference and try to exploit it. Naturally, the children of the privileged mother will consider themselves superior to those of the other family.

Once this feeling has been detected, it is time for the father to move in swiftly to foster better understanding between the children. Perhaps he should tell the proud child, 'It is dangerous to take things at their face value; there are some who are in the lead today, Christians say, who will come last tomorrow.'

If the child is proud because she is more beautiful than the daughters of the other mother, he might confront her, 'Do you know that the beauty of the heart is better than that of the body? There is a saying that, even though it is good to look beautiful and to look at beauty, beauty is not "eaten". So, the most important thing in life is to be a decent, kind, and loving human being.'

African religion

African religion has had tremendous influence in keeping the large family compact. The principles of the religion stress that it is not merely out of self-interest that one should do good to others, but also out of submission to the will of his own Creator. Because of having a common Creator, the outsider becomes an insider too. Furthermore, man is part and parcel of God's thought. It is common for the polite and religious Africans to tell people who have mistreated them, 'Never mind, God will see you.' In other words, God will punish the offenders on behalf of the offended.

It is dificult to separate a painter from his paintings in that the works of a painter are a manifestation of that painter. Likewise, the works of God must be seen as attributes of God and to respect and love them is to love God himself. According to African peoples, says Mbiti, man lives in a religious universe, so that natural phenomena and objects are intimately associated with God. They do not only originate from Him but also bear witness to Him.[25] The side of a universal moral order, of the ordering of forces, of a vital hierarchy, observes Father Placide Tempels, is very clear to all Bantu.[26] They are aware of that, by divine decree, this order of forces, this mechanism of interaction among beings, ought to be respected. They know that the action of forces follows immanent laws, that these rules are not to be employed arbitrarily. They distinguish use from abuse. They know that he who does not respect the law of nature is a man whose innermost being is pregnant with misfortune and whose vital power is vitiated as a result, while his influence on others is therefore injurious. This ethical conscience of theirs is at once philosophical, moral and juridical.

Since philosophy and psychology in traditional Africa is realised only when lived it can be deduced from the above argument that, the co-wife has a moral obligation towards the other wife. She and her children (that is taught to the children too) are not merely properties of a man she calls her husband, but she and the others are all subjects of another bigger whole—the Creator—who expects them to be fair to one another. And in turn, the Creator rewards the right doer and punishes the wrong doer.

This religious thought is not merely a philosphy of the old African, but the founding belief, manifest or clear, passed on from one person to another, which is at the heart of the common African of today.

Foundation for future living

The large family acts also as an excellent workshop for each sex to learn the nature of the other. Daughters are apt to benefit more than sons in polygamous homes. The daughters have their own natural mother, plus a step-mother. The double mother-brain-power at their disposal helps the daughter tremendously understand and find her position in the world. She is not merely the subject of the good and evil parts of one mother: her world is larger. What her own mother fails to teach her, the other mother does so. It is usually the step-mother who acts as the go-between between the daughter and her own mother in delicate situations. Hence, it is not unusual for the step-mother to hear of 'the boyfriend' or 'pregnancy' before the natural mother hears about it. This is because the daughter feels free, in this case, to communicate with her own parents through a person who is neutral. As the result of this comfortable arrangement, she is not likely to bottle up her psychological problems that might develop to destroy her life later.

It is also possible that in a monogamous union the daughter gets oppressed easily, much more if she has a mother who is dominating. This is the relationship that can easily bring about a breakdown of communication if the daughter finally becomes disillusioned with her own mother and reaches the conclusions that it is useless to try to put across her view to the mother. This development, no doubt, has adverse effects both to the daughter's future and to the daughter-family relationship.

What the daughter is not taught by her full sisters, she is taught by her half-sisters. The circle of her friends, which plays a big part in promoting better chances of marriage, is also larger than that of the daughter in a monogamous home, but the step-sisters and step-brothers too. She grows up in a richer social environment.

The plural marriage is also a great challenge to her in terms of bearing responsibilities. If she can succeed and make a name in this large family, she can be rest assured that she will do well in any other family.

The same can be said about the son in a polygamous marriage. He, too, has two mothers and can learn a great deal from their combined effort. Later in life when confronted with a marital problem, his wife's character shall first be reflected on his own mother naturally, then on his step-mother. His 'woman image' shall not be dominated by that of his own mother only (which may not be a good personality to emulate). He views his wife from different mirrors. The mirror of his own mother and that of his step-mother. This is advantageous and he is likely to make a more emotionally balanced husband than the son from the monogamous family. Naturally, he learns a lot about wives from his own father who lived with more than one wife. He, too, grows up with a healthy knowledge about the problems and blessings of a polygamous marriage and could, if necessary, become a polygamist with a fair degree of success.

Symbolically, monogamy stands for selfishness and polgyamy for generosity. As one African polygamist put it, a man with one wife can be compared to one with a Bachelors Degree; the second marriage can be seen as a Masters Degree in marriage and domestic affairs; the third marriage and onwards constitute a Doctor of Philosophy Degree in marital affairs and woman psychology.

Distorted views

The white missionary and the western civilization have been ambitious in interpreting African polygamy, but by giving or emphasizing the negative aspects. They have dwelt unreasonably on the economic side of the issue at the cost of the psychological and pragmatic side of life. Marriage is much more an emotional thing than it is economic. Indeed, since the world does seem to require more of a balanced person psychologically than economically, it is very important that the growing child should be given good and enough emotional tools with which to face this world for, as Christ put it, man does not live on bread alone. And as the Chinese put it: it is better to give a person a fishing hook than to give him a fish.

To the true man, the second wife is not merely an additional slave in his camp as many westerners have articulated. To him, that second wife is a God-given duty to bestow kindness and love upon yet another person. This explains why polygamy has been treated with religious feeling in traditional Africa, and this religious view may explain why there were always more wives in the homes of the noble and rich men. It was not merely the sexual urge and love of children that made a man want to have fifteen wives. Any sensible person knows that no single man can satisfy fifteen wives sexually. Neither did the wives take such a man for a husband with illusions of his sexual potence. At least, they were not such idiots as not to distinguish sense from nonsense. They married that man mainly because he was wealthy in moral food. Hence, he was a rock on which to build a permanent home.

The missionary and the whiteman misrepresented the African polygamist that he was obsessed with the number of women under his command; hence, his was a manifestation of greed but not an action guided by good sense and necessity. If we grant this thesis some plausability, what would these people say about those women who accepted so mutually to live under the command of one man? Such a thesis would try to make the African woman a thoughtless creature, which she has never been!

The general rationalization of the woman going into polygnous marriage is usually that, if that man can provide adequately for two wives, he is likely to do so for three. It can be argued that a man who can make five wives happy is almost guaranteed that he can make six happy. In most cases, it is the security and sense of belonging that woman goes for in polygamy.

That sexual part of marriage which has been given undue significance by whitemen who appeared either as critics or anthropologists, not to mention the missionaries, is but one arm of the body of marriage as it is known in Africa, an arm that is usually at the bottom of the list to be considered by a chief polygamist when he has to make his decision to marry the seventh wife.

The white missionary of the colonial days told the African that religiousness, or rather, the only way to heaven was having one wife, against the African's belief that a man immortalized his name and pleased his God more by marrying many wives and having many children. It is not difficult to imagine the amount of confusion generated by this cultural and religious contradiction.

However, whatever God's wish is, it cannot be far from the belief that, in both the earthly and heavenly kingdoms, the right way to live is to be laughing, singing, dancing, loving and marrying big for, as Christ put it, life is given to man so that he may live and have it, and have more of it in abundance.

The western Christian marital view is one of misery. Surely, it should be more Godly to give the so-called destitutes and illegitimate children, widows and divorcees, human sympathy and love, than to abandon them as unclean human beings, particularly the so-called children born in sin or illegally or unwantedly. There is nothing better to the human being than sympathy and love and those can come only from within man's genuine love for the whole child, his love for the whole human being based on the understanding of who man is and what his place and time is on earth.

CHAPTER TWELVE

Is Polygamy Dying?

Polygamy on the decline?

Many western scholars of anthropolgy and social sciences, including Christians, have repeatedly said in books, television and radio interviews and in seminars that the ancient African cow of polygamy is sick and is dying and, in the near future, it will die completely.

'If it dies,' reacted one African sarcastically, 'then we shall skin, roast and eat it if proven that it didn't die of anthrax which has not caught up with polygamy yet.'

This view of the death of polygamy has also been adopted by some Africans who have been influenced by the west and who believe that civilization comes only with monogamy.

But is it true that the good cow is going to die?

This question cannot be answered in one sentence. To answer it too, demands some scientific argument based on the study of human nature related to marital behaviour. But just before we proceed further, let us define the term *marriage*. The Oxford Advanced Learner's Dictionary defines marriage as, *an instance of legal union of a man and woman as husband and wife.*

The term *legal* in *legal union* poses a new comprehension problem. What is legal? Legal to whom and from what stand? In the apartheid South Africa, a black man who tries to live in a place reserved for white men, is regarded to have done so illegally by the white man. But is it illegal to the black man? It is then necessary to define the word *legal*. The same dictionary defines *legal* as *connected with, in accordance with, authorized or required by the law.*

Who makes that law?

Of course, that law is made by people who are empowered to rule the state. In other words, the state's authority takes what is right for legality and what is wrong for illegality. By no means is that law representative of every individual's view on the subject regarded as good or bad, right or wrong. What is legal, therefore, is mainly what conforms with the aspirations of ambitions (illusionary or otherwise) of the state. *Legal* is, by all means, a political term. And it is the politician who makes the law.

In a communist country, for example, marital law must reflect directly or indirectly the aspirations of communism. In a capitalist country, likewise, marital law must reflect the aspirations of capitalism. Marital law, or any law for that matter, is a manipulation of the state. If the capitalist or communist ambition is to live in Mars, the marital law should promote the progress towards Mars. All marital disagreements and child problems connected with the move to Mars should, therefore, be tolerated. If a single important woman in the struggle for settlement in Mars conceives and gives birth to a child which she murders because the said child is a stumbling block to her profession which is so dear to the nation, such murder is treated with lenience and understanding. Hence, she stands a better chance of being acquitted of the murder charge she faces so that she can be set free to go back to her work. These are the dynamics of law in the whiteman's world.

What is said about marriage in the whiteman's world is, obviously, coloured by politics. The whiteman's view on polygamy and monogamy smells of politics.

Point of departure.

In traditional Africa, marriage, like many other human institutions, has not been the subject of politics and national policies, at least, not in that conspicuous form. Marriage has been purely a language of survival, and it was let free to operate on the natural law of survival. An illiterate Maasai herdsboy, for example, knows more about the use of the steppe and vegetation of East Africa, observes Eugene Hillman, than does a western graduate in botany.[27] The science of marriage has been developed within the natural workshop of living and human requirements.

The question of whether polygamy will finally yield to monogamy in Africa is, for the above reasons, a political question from the cultural standpoint of the whiteman. If the move here in Africa is to adopt the western values then, obviously, the answer to the question would be different from the one arising from a situation in which the African has to maintain and promote his own cultural values both at the state level and at the level of the individual.

In an attempt to modify the colonial law of marriage to suit the African need, the Kenyan Parliament once found itself in a terrible fix. The most chaotic and violent scene erupted in the house when Members of Parliament attempted to find and pass a law against adultery in which, according to the view of some law makers, a person who was found guilty of adultery should suffer a six-month sentence in prison. But if such a law passed, cried other parliamentarians, it would bring the nation to a standstill.

Perhaps that argument was based on the realisation that every adulterous action involved a man and a woman. Hence, the couple should go to prison. Then the cries diversified, 'What happens if the court finds a father of ten children guilty and sends him to prison leaving them with no one to support them in a case where he was the only bread winner? Will the mother of the children, too, go to prison, and what will happen to her children while she is in jail?

But what in hell is this term, adultery?

The Oxford Dictionary definition of 'adultery' is, *a voluntary sexual intercourse of a married person with somebody who is not the person to whom she or he is married*. With this definition, the biblical law of Moses begins to ring out, 'Thou shalt not commit adultery.'

According to this definition, again, 'adultery' can be linked with western politics and the Christian concept. For that reason, the Kenyan parliamentarians found themselves in a precarious situation to define, in African terms, what actually 'adultery' means. The more they debated on the term, the more the term became elusive in an African context. For in Africa the situations are, by natural law and belief too, too complex to accommodate the term. Not to mean, of course, that the African is incapable of discerning adulterous behaviour from a legal one.

In that debate, the levirate case easily entered the argument. My brother's widow, they cited, do I ignore her needs, and is that in conformity with African religion and philosophy? Do I become more moral by ignoring her emotional needs? My old childless aunt has 'married' a woman in the hope that this woman shall give his home an heir; so, my aunt has begged me to impliment her wish by having a child with the wife: what do I do? Do I say no to the survival request of my aunt? What about the husband who lives hundreds of miles from his wife who cannot afford to bring his wife to live with to cater for his bodily needs; if that poor man is found having sexual intercourse with another woman, prostitute or otherwise, should he too, serve the six months of jail?

Eventually, they were forced to take the bull by the horns: in the present African setting, what are the circumstances that lead one to commit adultery? What are the conditions that lead a man into taking another woman for a second wife? Is it adulterous to go to bed with a woman who is a prospective second wife? Is it possible to wait sexually until she becomes a legal wife? How would the first wife naturally view the intentions of her husband when he is courting another wife for a second wife? Has he, according to the proposed penal law against adultery, a case to answer to her with regard to the imagined, intended, or already committed adultery?

In the end the controversial Kenyan debate became so 'adulterous' and messy that it ended in a dead-lock. The debate became not only ridiculous but unAfrican. They shelved it away perhaps until Kenya had attained the 'maturity' or rejecting African values and adopting foreign ones.

Understanding of marriage

In Africa, marriage is not an end in itself but a beginning of another whole. Here, the relationship between man and woman in a marriage is, in so many ways, a way of life. It is in the relationship between man and woman and the natural dependability of each other in material and emotional survival, added to the belief of an orderly world as presented by the Creator, that is totally responsible for making the right law on which their unity should operate. This relationship should not be tampered with by ideological or factory manufactured emotions and aspirations. Hence, in traditional Africa, man and woman relate to each other as closely as possible to the principles laid down by nature.

Polygamy is, indeed, a natural order.

It is naturally accepted that the marriage of two persons brings together two persons who are different and who may, or may not, cope with each other and deliver the fruits required of each other. African thought acknowledges how immature it is to believe in the western chorus of 'love that never dies.' For love can survive only when there are other factors that make life possible, as we saw in another chapter. And, just to emphasize that point, love, like fire, is possible and potent only when there is firewood. Love and marriage based on stringent regulations against extra-marital relations and polygamy, is blind to many natural realities and is usually vulnerable to future changes that deviate from the framework in which it was conceived. State law that reflects this weakness is responsible for social evils that may emanate from its society pertaining to the maladjustment of the sexes.

This is the view that makes the African marriage potentially polygamous. And one can conclude that as long as this basic philosophy finds room in Africa, the end of polygamy is still in the hazy horizon if not beyond, and far beyond. Western scholarship and its devotees have been advancing the theory that polygamy will diminish with advancing industrialization and urbanization fuelled by the statutory registration of marriage that is becoming more and more the way of recognizing marital status. But that contention is, at least most parts of it, very misleading.

There is an African proverb that tapeworms go to exile with the person. There are too many examples today that seem to confirm that, after all, polygamy is following the African across the cultural transition. If it does not follow him, it will simply change its face into that of the West—resolving on concubinage or what is popularly known in Nigeria as 'the outside wife.' This Nigerian term deines marital status of the modern hypocrite polygamist in two grades. The 'outside wife' and the 'inside wife.' An 'inside wife' is frequently, not always, an elite woman who has been married in a church wedding or through statutory law, usually both; this kind of marriage usually subscribes to the Christian ideology of monogamous marriage, at least as an ideal, explains Wambui wa Karanja in her study of the term.[17] In Nigerian local parlance, she is sometimes referred to, especially by the 'outside wives' as the 'ring' wife. She usually lives with her husand and their children in their 'official' residence. She adheres tenaciously to the western concept of love, affection, companionship and fidelity. An 'inside wife' is frequently suspicious and contemptuous of the 'single' women who are of marriageable age because these women constitute a constant threat to her monogamous marriage which is often in an uneasy equilibrium. Although the odds are against her, she prays and hopes that her marriage will be a rare exception; that hers will weather the storm when so many other monogamous marriages are so tumultous.

It is at the back of the mind of the 'inside wife' that, as said in many commentaries, evey husband harbours some polygamous intention, views, or emotions: therefore, she must be on the look out. She has seen and heard of so many polygamous marriages. Furthermore, the African law is not in support of pinning her husband down to monogamy. With that stance, she picks up her weapons and goes out to fight against polygamy in support of monogamy.

There is no concensus as to who, exactly, is the 'outside wife', even though the statutory laws and Christian forms of marriage are normally used to define an 'inside wife'.[29] A man who originally married under statutory law, or in a church wedding, subsequently, may decide to take an additional wife through native and custom law, although this is legally unacceptable. The 'church wife' may or may not (usually she does not) recognize the new 'wife' as properly married to her husband.

The 'inside' and 'outside' wives have been created by the state in its attempt to partly take side with western values. This happens to barely illustrate the confusion within the African State with regard to which way to go. But the man with polygamous blood, as the West sometimes describes him, still goes for his extra wife regardless of what name the outside world gives her—outside wife, concubine, prostitute, marriage wrecker (as seen by the 'inside wife'), girlfriend, lover or whatever.

It was earlier thought that higher education for the 'native' would rid the African man of his polygamous tendencies, so that with increasing level of education and 'civilization' awareness, the need to ban polygamy altogether from Africa would be appreciated. That, unfortunately, has not been the case. I contend that there is a definite upsurge in polygamy among the elite Nigerian men, adds Karanja, even though there is still an attempt to maintain a semblance of monogamy for public consumption.[30] This is not entirely contradictory because, as Banton has observed: while Africans often appear to imitate European ways, their cultural borrowing is in fact selective and the items taken over acquire a different significance in African culture.[31]

If in the English legal codes polygamy as an abberation, contends Chuma Ifendi of Nigeria, it is because England is a white homeland, very distant socially and culturally from the blackman's culture.[32] It is true that Britain ruled Nigeria sometime ago and left its codes behind as a legacy, but we have the right to be ourselves in the true spirit of negritude and the much publicised concept of African personality.

If polygamy is surely on its way out and monogamy is on its way in for permanent situation, what is obvious is that prostitution, concubinage, homosexuality, frequent divorce and abortion, just to mention a few of the evils, are going to be our legacy from Europe, America and elsewhere from the whiteman's world. All the same, it is nonsensical to think that the disappearance of polygamy is the appearance of civilization and woman's marital happiness; for if success and happiness have not come to the countries where monogamy is the rule, why should anyone here think that these will be the blessings of Africa when polygamy goes?

If only Africa could learn from the mistakes made by Europeans!

It has been claimed by the West that monogamy improves the position of woman and brings about sex equality. But that is at best a sweet but futile propaganda. In a society of marriage-haves and have-nots, one can't surely boast of sex equality. What we so often forget is that, when you dig a hole somewhere, you create a hill elsewhere with that soil. In Mars, man will still need food, love, and protection. These three are the primary colours of life and we should not be carried away by the secondary colours that we see.

A woman, any woman with full senses, would love to have a man for a partner whether for procreation or for something else. It is in man that a woman realises herself as a full human being, just as it is in a woman that a man realises himself as a full human being. What then happens if she cannot find that partner? One girl who had waited for a man for too long to come to her life got disillusioned and said, 'From now on, I am not going to attend anybody's wedding: I am weary of going to weddings to see other girls getting married when no man wants to marry me!'

The western countries have developed fantastic political theories on the dangers of situations that produce the 'haves' and 'have-nots.' Their lectures say that it is the struggle between the two that creates robberies, political unrests, industrial strikes, labour exploitation, oppression, corruption, alcoholism, drug addicts and so on. The thesis is that the

144

oppressed is driven into the criminal world in his trial to escape from his oppression and wretched life. It is unfortunate that this theory of the 'haves' and 'have-nots' is not, in that world, seen in the light of the single lonely woman vis-a-vis the married woman. Theirs is a setup that seems to assume that if a woman has access to employment and material world of men, she, needs very little else to make her happy. In that world, marriage is taken by many as a matter of secondary importance. That is why the statement among warring couples 'I can live without you' is so popular. 'True,' it should be added, 'you can live without me, but, surely, you cannot live without another person somewhere else who is not me and in a world where you are alone.'

If the rich and the poor are not equal, surely, the married and the unmarried women are not equal to each other, let alone being equal to men. The lonely woman and the married woman are equal to each other in the sense that both share the same human features; however, they are very unequal when it comes to what they get for their emotional and physical needs. In this situation, the western woman is set against herself. For how can a person sit among starving persons and eat his own good meal in peace? He would either be robbed of the meal, or if he must eat it successfully at all, he must be armed to the teeth to keep off the hungry ones from taking his meal.

The 'have-not' woman, realising that she has to swim or sink, usually evolves her own way of survival which may not be necessarily a peaceful one. For, is it possible for her to say, 'Okay, there is no man for me, so let me forget all about men'? Darwin's theory of survival for the fittest becomes more of a reality in her world. So, come what may, through thick and thin or through hook, and crook, the single lonely woman sets out to find her own man among the men of other women. What morals does she carry with her in this business therefore? Who is her friend and enemy at this time?

In this frame of mind, obviously, she is at war with the married woman. She realises that she must fight it out for her own survival. The commander of that war is the man.

Psychologists and marriage counsellors know how many divorces have been caused by this fight. Churches know how many have lost their faith in this war. Children know the bitterness they have experienced in this war. Courts of law know how many victims of the war they have

145

received. And the parents can hear the 'sounds' of bombs in the battlefield where their children are bound for.

It is a sweet fallacy to think that a woman who is faced by all these problems is more liberated than the one who is not. Africa has been told that the western woman is not exploited by man. Is that true, given the situation in which she is perched? In that world, the wife consummates or is forced to consummate her marriage with a 'gun' by her side. The man of that world takes advantage of his position. He knows that he is worshipped by woman because he is the life giver. A man who knows that it is easy for him to marry another 'brand new' wife as soon as the present 'bad' one goes away, glows with the pleasure of self-importance and state of being privileged. In that situation, naturally he is inclined to be intolerant of his 'bad' wife's shortcomings. This is even more dramatic when he is intoxicated with the illusions from which most husbands suffer, that, this time, he would find himself a better wife who really understands him. Subsequently, he is likely to misuse his wife within the corridors of his statutory law.

There is a story told of one man who had discovered that the law would catch up with him if he did not 'disguise' the use of violence against his wife whom he wanted to get rid of in favour of what he thought was a more exciting young woman. So, he took to other forms of violence such as, for example, clearing his throat and spitting on her face, disapproving any effort she made, ridiculing her in public, ignoring her sexually and talking good about other women.

Result?

He succeeded because his most frustrated wife committed suicide.

The law never found out the truth as there were no physical proofs in support of her case. So, the husband married the exciting girl, but no one told us what became of that marriage thereafter and whether or not they lived happily.

The western law may appear comprehensive, but it is far from being that, particularly the law that defends woman. In the first place, because that law is predominantly made by men, consciously or unconsciously, to safeguard their own interests. It is said that when you educate the cow that the milk which is meant to feed her own calf goes to feed your child, the cow starts kicking when being milked. They say that there are many ways of killing a cat: there are many ways of subjecting woman to humiliation and violence in the western code of law.

In that world, the great harvester is the psychiatrist and the doctor, both of whom live by the catastrophies that are constantly manufactured and defended by the law of their society. The lesbian is forced into her situation by the imbalanced conditions of her world. The mistreated concubine is the victim of that culture in which other equally worse phenomena survive, including sexual perversion, women alcoholism, abortion, pornography, exploitation of woman by the rich and industrial promotions, child rape, sadism, and others.

Most of these evils enter the society because of the simple and primary fact that the society or the law, does not cater adequately for the need of all women in spite of the glittering propaganda of a civilization that should be exported to Africa. In a world where women are not equal to one another, it is inevitable to develop a situation in which the psychological balance of the single mother is highly affected. The child that grows up in that society, therefore, becomes a victim.

In a polygamous community, the value of woman is high because there are hardly any second or third-class women. All women, except witches, are important persons. This is because the surplus number of women who would otherwise distabilize other marriages and frustrate the married women, has dissolved into polygamous relations with men who value having more than one wife. The widows go to the sympathetic and responsible men, relatives of the dead husband. The polygamy world is not a world of survival for the fittest woman. Where will the prostitute come from when all the women are married? Where will the homosexual come from when all the men have been allowed a natural sexual expression through marriage, and when they, as children, have been brought up in a society that does not preach competition or rivalry among women for marriage and social acceptance?

Sexual frustrations in particular, are responsible for making psychopathic societies. If the dynamics of polygamy are fully employed in Africa today:

(a) Africa will need less man-power in psychiatry, less doctors and less prisons. The medical world tells us that better care of the psychological needs of a community could, drastically, reduce the number of patients and deaths in that community because a good number of these physical diseases and accidents stem from psychological problems.

(b) There will be less cases of abortion and child abuse emanating from unwanted pregnancies.

(c) There will be less crimes that are sexually and maritally motivated.

(d) Male chauvinism will be minimized.

(e) There will be less sexually transmitted diseases.

(f) There will be more loving and dedicated parents, and less children, if any, who will be discriminated against on the basis of illegitimacy.

(g) There will be less women and young girls subjected to man's deceiption as inspired by economic strength and competition for marriage among women. More and more girls will settle down to their education because the pressure of getting married shall be less.

(h) More and more women will respect their own sex without feeling that they are unlucky because they were born females.

(i) There will be more people with more self-confidence, faith in nature and God and with respect for life as a whole.

(j) Tnere will be less marital disagreements and quarrels based on obsessive jealousy and fear of divorce. Less quarrels and more love brings up better psychologically balanced children; and balanced children and citizens create a sane society and high civilization.

And all these because one of the primary colours of life has been observed. To summarize it all, if Africa stands on its own philosophy, polygamy should live as it has always lived and for the betterment of the society. The African should ignore this philosophy only at the peril of his own civilization and survival.

The African should recognize this invaluable pillar of his old civilization. The pillar is the complete unity of man and woman, every man and woman, in the understanding that only through the interaction with each other can the life of this place retain its full meaning. Nothing in the world is more important to man than the love of woman even though some men may not be consciously aware of this. And nothing is more important to woman than the love of man, again, even though some women may not be consciously aware of this. For woman and man constitute the beginning

148

and even the ending of human life as we know it. Once that natural law has been tampered with by either frustrating man or woman from expressing himself or herself naturally through the other, the greatest balance of life has been disturbed and disaster should be expected.

Birth, copulation, and death, these are the basic facts of human existence, says Eugene Hillman, as summarized rather succinctly in 'The Four Quarters' of T.S. Eliot.[33] There is, to be sure, much more than this to be said about the human experience, but nothing less can be said.

The founding wisdom for the creation of an ideal civilization is contained in the allowance of a free flow of contact between man and woman; and once that has been observed, the rest finds its own course like water flowing through the field.

CHAPTER THIRTEEN

The Prospective Second Wife

Polygamy and the single girl

These days many people make big noise about the need for material employment. But very little is said, if any at all, about the rising moral unemployment. Newspapers have been printing bold headlines about the lack of city accommodation, condemning mothers for feeding their babies with the bottle, casting curses upon prostitutes because they are seen as unwanted human beings, and so on. Once in a while, some governments come up with 'illiterate' moves in which, for example, they arrest city prostitutes and other 'suspicious' single and unemployed women, then transport them to the countryside as if the countryside were the dumping ground for the city bad woman. The thesis is that these are the bad elements that spread immorality in the city. However, when these bad elements are transported to the countryside, they are not told what to do, or rather what their alternative is. The first important question to ask is, what have the countryside folks done to warrant all the prostitutes being dumped upon them? Or rather, what are the ethics of sending prostitutes back to the countryside? Of course the obvious answer is that the authorities look upon the parents of those loose girls to discipline them. This expectation is built upon the general misconception that girls take to prostitution because they are disobedient or because they have not been properly brought up. But whereas this may have some contribution to the problem, such is really an oversimplification of the issue.

In the first place, to send them to the countryside is to engage in an indirect promotion of prostitution. What will the prostitute do when she gets there? Obviously, offer herself to the countryman for money too. She will go after the husband of the rural wife. She will interact with the rural wife and while talking to her, the prostitute shall justify herself by emphasizing the fruits of being a 'free person without a man in the name of husband beating me up and breathing over my shoulder at my work always.' If she is persuasive, she is likely to deceive many.

In the meantime, the city law has relaxed and now the exiled prostitute can return to the city where the trade is much better. But she returns to the city bringing with her her convertees. In other words, though not the intention of the authorities, the prostitute had been sent to the country side to recruit more of her likes.

It is foolish to condemn a person who has no alternative, particularly when the one who condemns does not offer a progressive alternative. I do not want to imply that prostitution is caused by the fate of girls who do not find men to marry; that is only one of the many reasons that bring about prostitution.

However, what should not pass unsaid is the kind of thought that invade the mind of the frustrated, single and lonely woman who is either discriminated against or despised and, at the same time, frequently misunderstood. It is so easy to conclude that a woman who has not found a man to marry is, therefore, a bad girl.

Such 'bad' girl usually finds herself faced with a series of personal questions, such as:

(a) Will there never be a man to marry me?
(b) What in hell is really wrong with me?
(c) How come that others get married but not me?
(d) What tricks do they use to get a man for marriage?
(e) Is it not unfair that other women have men to themselves while others have no one?
(f) Should I or should I not rob one of these women of a husband?
(g) What do I have in my hands and within my powers that I could employ to get myself a man?
(h) Where does one go to meet men—in bars, towns, nightclubs, big cities?
(i) What does one wear to attract men and can I afford it?
(j) How can I make myself most beautiful and irresistible to men?
(k) Perhaps I have been too conservative—shouldn't I throw myself out loose and see what happens?
(l) What has future for me in store—only this endless disappointment?
(m) What will my old age find me like?

(n)   Do I have anything for security?

(o)   **What is the meaning of life and why should one be born at all?**

In the background of these   questions many grave solutions have been reached particularly by those who found it difficult to take the stiff challenges of life. Some of those victims have been driven into suicide, theft, murder, abortion, drunkenness, heart attack, just to mention a few of them. The following poem captures the mood:

I bear the coffin
of my own miseries
alone
and I pass unnoticed
unheard
even though I cry aloud and loudly
when I stumble and fall.

Some stare, then go
none offers me the land
upon which to dig the grave.

Here, every man, like every land
is curiously owned
except me . . .

I am the lonely owner
of the ship
that bears my miseries.
I sail through the sea of eyes
that don't see me.

Do you know? I invited many
to the burial of my miseries
but none came, I don't know why.
None replied, so
I shall dig the grave alone
with courage
till I reach
the deep wound of the ground.

I will need a shallow grave
just in case I fall into it
overcome
by the weight of the coffin
even though I don't think
anyone will miss me
if I die.

So, the problems of the single lonely girl are her own corpse to bury, and the sooner she realises this the better. Better if she faces the problem squarely, in a mature approach. There is no need of blaming her God for not giving her a man for marriage. May be the man is tucked under some corner she has not been to. He may not exist in the form he appears in her dreams; dreams are dreams and do not make the dreamer a millionaire simply because he has dreamt he was one.

Her man may be a widower, a bachelor, a polygamist, elderly or young, local or foreign, if only she could have courage. Life is a battle in which only those who fight and fight well (unless they have people to fight for them) have chances of better survival. The single lonely girl can do something positive about getting rid of the loneliness; it has been done by others; she can do it too.

On the other hand it would be too idealistic to gear everything towards marriage. In a way one can say that there is more to life than marriage. The other question to ask is: are we all born to marry and procreate? The answer is obviously no, but the debate may remain on the number that takes no for the answer. The traditional thought that the girl is brought up for marriage and procreation is faced with some new challenges in the new world. It is only too good to remember that we are born to live in the future and not in the past. Life styles are always forced to change with changing traditions, and no culture can ever remain static.

It is not true that all the unmarried girls are lonely and unhappy. Neither is it true that all the married women are happier than the unmarried ones. For example, the girl who has decided to serve her God as a nun, or get 'married' to Christ as they put it sometimes, may obtain full satisfaction in her life and may not experience loneliness. Today there is also the new girl who is too absorbed in her profession to be lonely and to miss marriage that much. There is another one who has turned back a

153

number of proposals which she feels or thinks or knows are not good enough, so she does not feel lonely. And there is the other who, for one pathological reason or other, feels that marriage is out of the question. Simply, let all these girls be excluded from the class of the lonely and unhappy because they have something worth to live for. It is the girl who feels deeply in herself that happiness depends upon getting a man for marriage, whom we are mostly concerned with here.

However, some warning must be sounded upon the girl who decides to 'marry' her profession simply because, for the time being and as far as things stand, the profession is everything. There have been many cases where the girl felt that she had, actually, made a big mistake right from the beginning by 'marrying' her profession. She discovers that she ought to have approached life from the natural path—that of marrying a man. Such disillusionment comes much later in her life when she has lost most of her prime attraction. But all the same, any choice of life is subject to disappointment and disillusionment.

There is the saying that trees do not grow from the sky; and this can be linked with any anticipation of happiness that is not founded on natural law. There are far too many dangerous paths in the way of life but, so far, the natural path is the one with minimum risks and no doubt the most satisfying of them all. We can fight against nature as much as we want, but nature seems to win all the time. There are certain basic requirements of a normal human being. By all means, good profession cannot be a substitute for a woman's desire to be loved by man. In other words, material things in whatever form, need to be complemented by the love of the opposite sex in order to make a bearer realise the joy of life fully. Homosexuals and lesbians may not buy the thought of love from the opposite sex, yet the symbolism is inherent in what they get from the other partner.

A person who is not sure of himself or herself should, therefore, always endeavour to chose the natural path. It should also be said that, at times, it is a weakness and dangerous to be too sure of oneself particularly in following the unnatural course. Any time is not too late to regret a decision that was unnatural; but hardly anyone with good brains regrets having taken a natural decision.

So often, what prevents people from doing better and living a more rewarding life is that unreasonable over-sensitivity and fear of 'what others will say.' A girl who is contemplating being a second wife, is usually under terrible emotional turbulence over what others will think about her. She feels strongly that, for sure, hardly anyone will appreciate her decision. In that situation it is difficult for her too, to find anyone to advise her on what to do. The psychiatrist and social workers we have today (who are also scarce anyway) who could help her reach a sound decision, have trained against the aesthetics of polygamy.

'Marry him at your own risk,' is the kind of advice she is likely to get from many of her friends, or the kind of repeated warning at the back of her mind. If she happens to harbour Christian values, along with that warning, she begins to wonder whether or not she would be breaking a Christian law by becoming a second wife. At the same time, she fears that by offering herself to a married man, she loses her personality.

It is within the hands of this dilemma that many unpleasant things can happen to her in her most desperate situation. As the saying goes, a drowning person clutches on straws. She can so easily land herself in a really dangerous position as, in desperation, people have been known to do anything.

Facing herself

A lot of this worrying could be avoided if the single girl realised that people will also say something nasty about her if she does not get married. Either path she follows, mouths will track her. People seem to live by gossiping about others as gossips, they also say, sweeten tea. She faces the problem more maturely if she keeps in her mind the fact that nobody can live on her behalf. It is said that nobody can stop birds from flying above the head, but he can stop them from laying eggs in his hair. She could actually stop those people from laying their negative faith in her heart.

Many girls miss their chance of marriage because of waiting for Mister Right, as Wambui wa Karanja puts it.[34] Mr Right holds, at the very minimum, a first degree. He is 3 to 5 years older than the girl; should preferably be from the same ethnic group and should have a discernable potential for future success; and he must be a bachelor.

The university graduate single and lonely girl is excellent material but she is not alone. There are so many others like her in the cross-section of girls, from the illiterate to the most educated. Quite a number of university graduates have lately found themselves threatened by an 'empty' future because they could not bring themselves to being second wives. Of course, it is much better if she can get herself a single man, but as the proverb says; when the lion fails to catch a prey it eats grass. It would be worse for her to choose the harder way when there is a less hard one. Is it better, she should ask herself, to face an 'empty' future than to be a second wife of some man?

The claim that monogamy as a form of marriage is better and more successful than polygamy is not true. The world has witnessed many bitter and murderous monogamous marriages. There are many happy and successful polygamous marriages in Africa and in other parts of the world. We all enter the ship of marriage with the best of intentions, monogamously and polygamously, but many of these marriages do not reach the destination. I think what matters most is the kind of relationship each wife develops with the husband. The idea of sharing a husband with another woman scares many women, but in practical living things can be different. One pragmatic wife of a polygamist gave her philosophy as: 'Actually, I can't help sometimes getting upset knowing that my husband is sleeping with another woman, but then I tell myself that the other woman is not just a woman. She is his wife and has just as much right over him as I have. I can't compare his relationship with her with those husbands who run with other unmarried women behind their wives' back. To me, my husband's other wife is simply a companion. We are often faced by the same problems. For example, when my husband's business is not going well, we both are worried. When he is ill, we meet at home to arrange how we are going to care for him. When he had an accident some few months ago, we both sat at his bedside tormented by the same thoughts.

'Our problems are common. When he goes abroad, we both escort him and both go to meet him when he comes back. It does not matter that we come in different cars. We both come with the children and, if anything, these are things that bind us together, especially the children. They love each other so much that they do not even seem to understand that they do not have the same mother. They call us both, mother.'

Faulty beginning

Sometimes the novelty of marrying a man for a second wife is centred on the expectation that the younger wife (or new broom sweeps clean) will get a better 'love fruit' than the first wife, but that is not always the case in practical living. Each wife is, of course, different from the other and carries her own special features. So, the younger wife does not necessarily have to command the larger part of the husband's love simply because she is so new.

'Traditionally the younger wife is supposed to be the favourite,' explains a co-wife in an article by Charles Otieno, 'but I cannot say that is strictly the case with us. If hers is a better house, mine is enough for me and the children. Hers is big and proportional to the number of children she has. We both drive our own cars and our children go to the same schools. Of course, some of hers are in secondary schools, but I know that mine will go to equally good ones. We both have our shares of businesses to run and also each of us has a farm. Since we are independent of each other, the tension is minimal. We only mix when there are occasions like weddings and funerals. But we are friends and comrades.'[39]

A girl who has faith in herself and is loving, can develop a sound and satisfying relationship with a man who is already married. After all, he marries her because he loves her, and his wish to marry her is an indication that there is a certain deficiency in the first marriage. There is, therefore, room for her. If she works hard, who knows, she might become his favourite wife!

The right man for polygamy

It is not possible to give the single girl very definite guidelines regarding who the right man is for polygamy. This is partly because human nature is diverse and people operate on individual tastes. However, there are some general things she could observe in order to minimize her risk. One of those things is that she should apply some common sense and substantial observation before she takes the man.

She should be very careful with a man who paints a most grim picture of his first wife. Such is a simple tactic many men employ when they want to deceive or exploit a firm girl. The 'grim' painter feels that if he makes a direct confession that his first wife is not that bad, the girl is not going to accept him. So, he tries to present himself as the unhappiest husband who is married to the wrong woman.

'Why do you think I could be better than her?' the girl may ask him.

'Because you have better vision than my wife,' he may advance, 'My wife is so extravagant! My wife is so careless! My wife is so unsociable! My wife is so unambitious! My wife does not know how to cook.'

It would be wise for the girl to investigate these allegations. What she should also know is that, if that is really how his wife behaves, it is possible that he may be pushing her in one way or another to act like that under some frustrations. The best cook can easily give up her effort if whenever she does her very best, the husband does not show any appreciation. She may be unambitious because she sees no way out to express her ambition and wishes. She may be extravagant because he, too, is extravagant. She may be an alcoholic because she is trying to cope with marital frustrations.

Men who are likely to be successful polygamists, ironically, are those who are successful with their first marriage. Unless the need for the second wife was brought about by a terrible problem with the first wife connected with witchraft or bad behaviour for example, one of the qualifications traditional Africa considered important was that the first wife of the man must look and testify that she is satisfied. Only then would the parents of the girl of the prospective second wife, consider the man for a son-in-law. It all worked on the belief that if he had been able to satisfy his first wife, he had enough moral and material property for a second wife.

Thorough investigation was conducted on how this man handled his children, relatives, neighbours, friends, old people and in-laws. Did he have some noble qualities? It was his sound quality of leadership as the head of his family that convinced the girl that this was a good man for marriage. Even in the case of inheriting widows, the person entrusted with the home of the widow had to be an emotionally mature man, otherwise the widow had to go to someone else.

There is a lot of security offered by this traditional approach. The first wife is really the guinea-pig of the second marriage. A husband who mistreats and ignores his first wife, is a wrong man for polygamy. Of course, investigations should also be conducted on whether the cause of his crude behaviour is provoked by his wife. It has been long known that a man's inside and outside behaviour has sometimes a lot to do with the kind of wife he has.

These days, the single girl contemplating being a second wife tends to be attracted to the man who is unhappy with his first wife. She expects that, perhaps, he would eventually divorce the first wife and create full room consequently, for the second wife. That attraction becomes even stronger if the man has implied in some way that he might consider divorcing his wife. Traditionally, the girl would face him with the question, 'Why then do you think I would be a better wife when I am simply a woman like your first wife?'

That kind of question attracts many deceptive answers today. When there were no big salaries, high and university education, women tended to be equal. But today with the introduction of material things, the cheat can easily reply, 'Because you are better educated than my wife. Because you are an intellectual. Because you come from an enlightened world. Because you are a progressive person.' It is common behaviour for many men not to tell why they want to marry the girl. They hide behind all kinds of emotional covers. A man who is looking for a woman with a big income to help him further his economic kingdom would still hide under the 'love' cover. He can't be honest enough to say, 'One of the things that make me attracted to you is the fact that you are a woman with an income and that is what I think I need desperately these days.' Such a confession would betray the idea of love. That is why he decides to keep silent about it and pretend that money is not actually the most important issue that influences his decision.

The same thing can happen with girls too. She can't admit, 'I want to marry you because you are wealthy.' Human nature has it that, in most cases, the real motive for interaction—be it in marriage or in another relationship—is too personal or embarrassing to be expressed openly; so it is much better kept tightly as a personal secret and as long as it is possible, sometimes as long as one lives. So, one part of human nature is that, so often, we live with people whom we actually do not know thoroughly even though they may be intimate friends and lovers, husbands and wives.

Since the material world has made it possible for everybody to camouflage one's true feelings more efficiently, the girl interested in a second marriage must do some good home-work about the man she is prospecting. She should be careful not to embrace him simply because of his love poetry. Such poetry can be learned anyway. Or she should not rush at him because of his expensive car. Unless he is a cheat, a man who is going for a second wife for a noble reason is usually down-to-earth.

The man and his money

Most second marriages take place when the man is already well established in either his business or profession. Hence, he cannot be economically compared with the bachelor who came from college the other day, who has worked for a short period and is still struggling with buying beddings, furniture, clothes, utensils and so forth. Such man outweighs the bachelor in material things and is much more sophisticated. He has bought his furniture already, has perhaps bought himself a piece of land and put up a handsome home in the countryside. Hence, he has become a man of assets. If he belongs to the middle class *tissue* he has most likely bought himself a car, or even two—the other one driven by his wife.

Such man is in an enviable position. He is irresistible to the single poor girl. In this man, she sees many things which could make her live happily—money, clothes, handbags and perfumes, home, security, prestige and so on. Perhaps the man is in an influencial position to get her a job just like that. So, this is not just a man: he is many good things and the door to better life.

But unfortunately, he has another wife!

A classic example is the boss's poor secretary. She has been rubbing her shoulders with this powerful man who has been promoting her, or who is in a position to promote her. She admires him for what he is and what he has. He has been making curious remarks or complaining about his wife who the secretary knows already. The secretary is already aware that her boss is unhappy with his marriage because of one thing or other. He has been making some advances and she feels very vulnerable. Certainly, this man could change her life for the better. Finally, she submits to him.

Any accumulation of material things takes time. The man and his wife got all that at the expense of sweat and waiting, having started from zero. Obviously, even when the husband does not admit it, the wife must have had a big share in the building of that stack. It is at this stage that the girl meets the man and falls in love with him.

It is dangerous to base her decision on his affluence. Many wealthy men are mean with their money. If he is rich but there is no evidence of his riches in the way his wife is kept, it is much better for the girl to keep off even when he promises to allow her to carry his cheque book. If he owns a car that his wife does not drive, the girl should not think quickly that she would have access to that car even though he might have promised her to drive it, or to use it to teach her how to drive. If he only intends to teach her driving, a more pragmatic approach would be to pay for her driving lessons before the marriage.

She can expect with utmost accuracy that what he does to his first wife is what he will do to the second wife!

The girl should not be deceived to think that she can come to that home and take over the control of his finances and business easily and overshadow the first wife just because he complains about her.

Before making any move, she should get it quite correctly what it is that actually makes him want to have a second wife. The reason must be convincing and practical. What he says should be thoroughly counter-checked by some form of communication not only with the first wife, but with the other relatives and friends of his.

It is not usual today that the man would give the girl access to any form of communication with the first wife in the formative stages of their relationship. That can even remain unchanged up to the last stage. The psychology of a man who is looking for a second wife is that his first wife is likely to stand in his way to try whatever she can to frustrate the effort in one way or other, unless both husband and wife were in mutual agreement right from the beginning to secure a second marriage. For that reason, he ignores her and he has the guts of telling the girl, 'It is my own life I am talking about: it is me you are going to marry and not my wife. I am the architect of everything and I shall have the marriage the way I want it.'

Whereas that may be true to a certain degree, things do not usually work out that way in practice. A girl who marries a man for a second wife, sooner or later, realises that she did, in fact, 'marry' the first wife in one way or another.

The woman who 'founded' that man the girl has taken, has certainly a lot of power over him although, naturally, he might not want to admit it!

First wives are usually very powerful and, in so many instances, continue to wield that power as long as they live. The second wife must be prepared, once in a while, to play a secondary role in the marriage. Tradition has it that the second, third and fourth wife, should refer to the first wife as 'Mother', mainly to acknowledge her position in this home. No first wife expects to be eclipsed and ruled by a wife who came to this home the other day. She treats the second wife as a newcomer and that is how it should stay.

The advice of the first wife

One time a girl fell madly in love with a powerful, wealthy man I knew who had two wives already. At that time, the man was a cabinet minister in the government of Kenya. From the manner in which this man behaved towards the girl, she was so convinced that he loved her. Her exciting dreams stretched out even further; she thought he had never loved another woman the way he loved her. She was going to marry him, and she was dying with the prospect of being a cabinet minister's most beloved wife.

Somewhere within the course of the courtship, a friend of hers advised her to have a word with the man's first wife. Arrangements were made without the knowledge of the big man. The beautiful, smooth, English-speaking girl finally found herself before the big Mama. The Beauty told her love story while the first-wife listened patiently, apparently, taking the matter lightly. When it was the big Mama's turn to speak, she told the Beauty, 'If I were to advise you, I would tell you not to marry my husband.

'Why'? she asked anxiously.

'I know him,' she added politely. 'I have lived with him for many years. I married him even before you were born.'

'So what?' she snapped.

'That's all.' The big Mama saw the love fire in the girl and knew that any further dialogue against the marriage would make the girl more suspicious of the Mama's motive. She would think that the Mama was merely out to play the bad game usually played by wives to guard their good husbands from the 'wolves.'

'You seem to be so much in love with him,' said the Mama finally, 'and very sure of every movement you make. Surely, I know that he loves you. But I can assure you that you are choosing a very rough course for your young life. Go ahead and marry him, since you do not seem to be prepared for any good advice.'

The Beauty did exactly that. She married the minister and enjoyed a number of privileges and trips overseas before he showed her his true colours. By then, she had a child. Now her eyes opened and she began to see that, apparently, the Mama had been very right. This was a beast, she found out; and this beast was already courting another foreign girl for a wife. He had become very touchy, and had very little time for the Beauty and her child not to mention the violence he deployed when angry. The Beauty felt awfully stuck. In the first place she did not have any employment, she did not have any profession and, to make matters worse, she had married this man against the advice of many people. Her own mother had been terribly against the marriage. Who would sympathize with her situation now?

One day when she had received a good beating and threats of being thrown out into the cold, she went to the Mama for advice. The Mama, as usual, listened patiently to the story of this young woman's marital bitterness. This time the Mama took it with humour and told the young wife, 'Give yourself more time to cry your tears out; take your baby and go back to your husband. As I was not there in your marriage deal, I would like to remain outside it. Now you might begin to understand how much I know the man. But more has to befall you yet. For the time being, I advise you stick to him but do not persuade me to try to talk to him. He listens to younger wives more than to old Mamas like the one talking to you now. So, if you do not mind, I would like to retire to bed now.' She was on her feet already.

The bitterness, or most of it, could have been prevented if only the girl had been more sensible and patient to listen to what the first wife had to say. Or if she had included the mama in the strategy of her marriage.

Irrespective of her intellectual aptitude, the first wife is bound to know the husband a great deal. The girl interested in the man should make use of that knowledge. In fact, she is in a better position to deal with a man who has been researched into quite well by another woman. If she takes him with that knowledge, she is likely to adjust herself to the marriage fast. Many girls go through a hell of trouble with their first marriage before they can grasp the right approach to the man. The second wife comes to walk on a path that has been cleared by another woman.

If the girl takes good time to 'read' the man from those who know him already, she stands a better chance of succeeding in the marriage. The trouble with many girls who are out for this form of marriage is that, they think, whatever the first wife says about the husband is merely to sling mud at him in order to scare the girls away. It is true that many first wives can do exactly that; however, if the girl is smart, she can still extract the truth from other sources.

It is recommended that, where possible, the girl should try to have audience with the first wife, with or without the approval of the man. If the first wife is approachable (many wives are not) the girl should go for advice from her. She should confess that the man has proposed to marry her and she is tempted to accept him, but as yet she is not quite sure what kind of a man he is. If she can get direct answers from the first wife, she should exploit the situation and get as much information about him as possible. If she has passed that stage well, then she should ask for a second meeting with the husband present.

In the case of the unapproachable first wife, the girl can make use of other persons whom she trusts to discuss the matter well with the first wife. This is usually the best method for laying down the foundation. Naturally, the messenger is direct and free from many constraints and can extract a lot of information from the first wife. He or she can argue freely in favour of the girl. This is why the traditional method of sending relatives, friends, or parents to introduce the matter was so effective and carried the least dangers.

The girl should not be in a hurry to get the man. It is a matter of security for her life. So, she should walk very, very carefully.

Testing the man

It is not enough that the girl finishes the deal with the man and goes ahead with the marriage. In Africa, people are owned by others. That is, nobody is wholly independent. In Africa, courtship is not a mere event in which a man and a girl recite the poetry of how much they love each other. The courtship is a big process or courting everybody in the background of the lover. As one put it, the background people should not be ignored in one's way to marriage because they may be needed in the keeping of that marriage, or on one's way out of that marriage.

When she has married the man she discovers that, practically, she married not only the first wife, but the children of the first marriage, the man's relatives, and also the relatives of the first wife! She marries an institution, not a single person, and there is no shortcut to that as long as she lives in Africa where the extended family is the key to stable living. As the proverb goes, he who buys a cow buys its cowdung too.

In testing whether the man means business, tradition has imposed the bride gift. The man who accepts the pains of paying the bride price proves that, indeed, he holds the girl at high value. It is not so much the material gain received that matters, but the 'heart-signature' that the man means business.

In the absence of bride price, the girl is left at a loss to assess the honesty of the man as the mouth is known to say many things that the heart does not mean. Yet, somehow, she must obtain some substantial evidence that the man really wants her. But one must not let it sound as though the bride price was a thing of the past. Even up to now, bride price is observed in many societies.

Regarding the modern approach, giving the girl presents and making fantastic promises is not enough. Any man can do these things to a woman he wants to deceive. There are far too many who pose as being in great need for a second wife when actually all they want is to have a good time with that girl and abandon her as and when it becomes necessary to do so. So, the girl must be extra-careful with a man who has another wife.

It is good if she uses the time of courtship to clear the doubts of her own relatives with regard to whether he is a genuine person or not. She should say 'yes' only when she knows for sure that a good number of her people are behind the decision. Besides, she needs the backing of the man's relatives too. For this reason, she should try as much as possible to desist from making any move to take the man until she feels that there are some people in his family who welcome her. Such is the healthy situation second marriages thrive on.

If she believes in bride price as a proof of his commitment, she should surely let the man pay it before the marriage. By no means should she 'sell' herself cheaply, or make the man feel that she is dying to marry him. Even if she be dying, she should try as much as possible to be 'thriving.' Otherwise, if she sells herself so cheaply, later during quarrels and fights, it is so easy for the man to hit back, 'After all, you were dying to marry me—I thought I did you a great favour by marrying you.'

Faking love and commitment

Girls have become very cheap these days. A man can lure a grown-up girl into marriage by simply reciting some Shakespearean lines to her and bribing her with some small presents and a dinner party. Western civilization tell us that you can meet a girl in the street, date her, and complete the engagement and marriage deal at a park then go home in the afternoon with the design of the wedding cards. Those may not be the words, but the symbol is expressed by the words.

If the girl's attempt to reach the first wife has been frustrated by one thing or other, either by distance or cultural differences in the case of inter-ethnic polygamy, she could choose to write to her. In that case, she should write as comprehensively and honestly as possible or simply ask for her audience. There are extremely few successful second marriages that did not consider the first wife. When the second marriage has taken place and is confronted with a series of problems that the man cannot solve easily, he may take refuge in the first wife and abandon the second one as many men have done from time to time. The girl should know, that the man she is interested in has another wife he could easily turn to if the second wife did not 'behave' herself.

Quite a number of polygamists do make use of the first wife too, to discipline or get rid of the second wife in case the second wife has become unmanageable. This is why the girl should collect as many signatures as possible to her application from both sides so that, when things go sour later, the signatories may come to her defence. It is usually the second wife who sits on the weaker branch in that marriage. Many men go for the second marriage with high hopes only to get disillusioned and return fast and with tears to their first wives.

If the first wife resists the marriage, it does not mean that the girl should give-up. The first wife, in other cases, can be a real danger to her life and that is why the girl must move very carefully. Best if the girl can get it all clear concerning her private accommodation and property. If possible, she should make sure that she has a profession or permanent employment just in case things backfire. Actually, she should be as independent as possible from the first wife. It is wise also to come to the marriage prepared to work for it hard and, if possible, make friends with the first wife. She should endeavour to accumulate her own property. The thought of inheriting easily what the man has accumulated with the first wife is, indeed, a bad dream. The first wife had to wait for a long time before she accumulated what she has, so why should the second wife get it so easily? Such is the rationale behind any disagreement over material things between the wives.

Why should the second wife try to woo the first wife?

One reason is that the first wife, in spite of her crude relationship with the husband, if such be the case, is still quite influencial in as far as the husband's decisions for the future are concerned. The second wife can make better use of the first wife's command over the management of the husband.

The senior wife is the library of the junior. When the junior is faced with big problems concerning how to handle the husband, it is good to remember that her senior has most of the answers; that is why it is to her own interest too to co-operate with the senior.

CHAPTER FOURTEEN

Concubinage

How to handle the concubine

A concubine is a woman who lives with a married or unmarried man as if she were his wife, without being lawfully married to him. This kind of woman is more or less a modern phenomenon in Africa, brought to Africa by the influence of western civilization.

I am simply being daring in handling this theme because any discussion that presents the concubine in a favourable light is bound to raise many eyebrows and create controversy. This is because concubinage is one of the 'untouchable' subjects by the 'clean.'

People know that concubines exist and are, indeed, a fact of life at least in the modern world, and they have their definite positive contribution to life. Yet they do their very best not to talk about them. But this silence is only a display of the hypocrisy that exists in people at all levels. A considerable number of men in academia would look 'askance', explains wa Karanja, at a public declaration by one of their members that he has an 'outside wife.'[36] I think this is due to hypocrisy than to inherent disapproval of such liaisons. In fact, a man with an 'outside wife' is usually secretly admired and admired by academic men generally.

The church does not want to talk about them except when cursing them as evil persons. The society and the law as a whole are harsh to the concubine. The concubine does not seem to have any position in public, she exists only in the background. In other words, she is the underdog of the modern community.

The polygamous nature of man keeps the fire of concubinage burning. To nearly every potent man, one woman is far from being enough. Forced by social or economic and other pressures to keep one wife with him, he begins to walk secretly in search of or dreaming of another woman.

'Since I was married at the age of twenty six,' relates one man in an article written by Charles Cinda, I must have watched, with great pain, at least half a dozen precious women, who could have been mine, quietly drift away from my life, all because I bore the ugly stigma of a married man. Some are married now; others have moved out of town and I never see them. I still remember them with bitterness, for I did hold and kiss them for a while before they were snatched away from me by the tentacles of this modern, unfair world. I still think of them as my women, for I had carefully sorted them out from the herd and given them my own invisible but indelible mark. Even when I meet them in the company of their husbands, I still see the mark; they blush and move on hurriedly as if afraid of that invisible, unpalpable tie that stil binds us. For they know too that, had we been living in other times, they would be mine and the husband would be a thief. Ask any honest man about my age and he will probably tell you the same—recount his losses while showing you the ugly scars of love fulfilled, then sacrificed at the alter for monogamy.[37]

The prostitute

What is the difference between a concubine and a prostitute? A dictionary describes a prostitute as person female or male, who offers herself or himself for sexual intercourse for payment.

From both definitions of concubine and prostitute, we can conclude that a concubine can also be a male person in the perimeters of homosexuality. But since homosexuality is not our concern here, we shall concentrate on the female concubine, by far the most common and oldest factor in man's and woman's relations. A concubine can be a prostitute, or rather, a prostitute can be a concubine, since both bear that which attracts men to them—sex appeal, that is, if sex is number one in the count of factors that attracts a man to a woman who is not his wife.

Circumstances that lead to concubinage

It would be wrong to flatly say that a concubine is a prostitute or a prostitute is a form of concubine of a short duration. Leaving the prostitute issue alone for a while, it is important to examine the circumstances that may lead a woman to become a concubine. Some of the leading reasons are:

    (a)   failure to get a man for marriage

    (b)   widowhood

    (c)   marital disappointment and divorce

    (d)   some socio-economic reasons

    (e)   natural disaster

    (f)   physical disability and pathological reasons.

From this analysis, we can see that the prostitute is a product of point (d). Therefore, prostitution is one of the many aspects of concubinage. The victim offers herself sexually for payment on different terms: on short, long or casual employment. And it is the duration of this contact and contract that determines the term to be used on the woman involved.

There are many reasons why a man goes to a woman even when he knows that she is a prostitute. It would be to over-simplify or promote misunderstanding of the issue to say that, that man comes to her for sexual release only. Using a Nigerian expression, let us simply say that sex is the 'soup' with which man-and-woman things are 'eaten.' He may come to her not because she is a prostitute or an easy lay, as some people put it, but because she is a likeable personality. Or she is someone who understands his needs better. Or someone who knows how to handle him effectively, physically and spiritually. Or someone who appreciates his thoughts or aspirations.

The view given by many people is that the prostitute is an evil, worthless, and foolish person. That is, indeed, not true always; or rather it is a grand generalization based on the assumption that people who have economic problems are irresponsible. Situations that may lead a woman to prostitution are many. In fact, some of them are noble, such as earning money to support her children because she has no other alternative.

Most prostitutes are decent persons with only an economic problem. But a distinction must be made between a mere economic problem and ambition, or greed to become rich through any possible means. There are some women who take prostitution as a profession and are therefore out to give it any art that is sure to capture the prey.

It is not easy for every woman to find a man for marriage these days, and it is not the wish of any wife to become a widow. Marital disappointments and divorces are human problems. There are many reasons that give rise to socio-economic problems. Natural disasters are

170

neither man-made nor woman-made. Physical and psychological diseases, disabilities and accidents are always waiting for us in all corners of life. And the undeniable truth is that no woman wants to be a concubine—events of life lead her into it. Given the choice, every normal woman would love to be married and earn the respect of married life.

Concubines in their many forms are, therefore, people in great need of help. But they are usually misunderstood and treated with great stigma. First and foremost, they are considered as thieves—some kind of moral thieves.

What does a concubine want?

Of course, a concubine is a woman who wants a man's company besides the other natural requirements. She is single and, as such, she is fighting against loneliness. She craves for a companion with whom to share the many tears and joys of life. She needs protection like any other woman. Man's protection. She needs physical and spiritual protection.

Whoever you are, it is always an exceedingly awful experience to feel that nobody loves and appreciates you. It is a pleasure, a great joy therefore, when a man comes to give her that love, any man, single or married. And her wish is that such love and appreciation she gets from this man should continue, if possible, for ever.

When the concubine gets engaged in a direct or indirect fight with the wife of the man who comes to see her, this fight should not be misunderstood. All women and men fight when their love is threatened. The concubine has the right to fight for her own existence, at least, that is how she sees things. Actually, she knows and understands her position in the society: that she is discriminated against. She knows that she is gravely misunderstood and her world is associated with immorality and hell. She is in a position that so easily and often, makes her feel that she is nobody and that life is, truly, too cruel to her as she is a surplus in the community. Usually she does not see any light for the future.

For all these reasons and others, she craves so much for the company of a man who can give her that sense of importance and appreciation that she is, in spite of all that she has done, a decent human being. She wants and expects to be forgiven for her sins, but not to be condemned. She

171

expects the community to see and understand her predicament and try to bail her out. She looks for support to her weak branch.

Hence, she is served best when the man tries to provide for her accordingly. His coming to her is, in a way, an indirect appreciation of her personality. She has a psychological wound that can be treated only by the man who comes to her. Others may misunderstand and abuse her, but not her man. Her man should appreciate her and try to help her be on her own feet emotionally. Her wishes and prayers are that this relationship should keep on growing from strength to strength.

Should the man not consider that?

Being human, with all the passions and weaknesses and dreams of a human being, she cannot afford, and should not be expected to do so, to love those who are out to take food from her mouth. Often, concubines are engaged in a serious move to undermine the marriage of men who come to them. The constant question that comes to her mind is, 'Why should he love that other woman but not me?' Her wish is that his marriage with that other woman should collapse. Or that other woman should disappear from the face of this earth. His wife is, naturally, her rival and her stumbling block.

Let us simply say that, after all, a concubine is only a name given to a woman whose relationship with man is of a different style; otherwise, all the things that the man does with his wife, he does with the concubine but in a different version.

In fact, she is a wife!

A wife of a lesser degree. According to Christ's statement whatever woman a man takes to bed, he has thus made her his wife. Strictly speaking, then, the concubine is a wife too. The man who comes to her is no more than a polygamist. Should the concubine, therefore, not be treated with respect and, indeed, with a sense of equality to his first wife? Is she not an important person to his life?

One can contend that if his wife was such an all-rounder or that perfect as she quite often sees herself, would her husband go to the concubine? Why does he go to her? Because of greed? His going to the concubine is a distinct proof of a deficiency in his wife, no more and no less. He brings to her the problems that his wife has not been able to solve. Okot p'Bitek has better words to explain it in his poem, *Two Songs*:

And you
My married sister
You whose husband
I also love dearly
When will you learn
To be grateful
To me?

When you turn
Into bloody bitch
And he storms out
Of your house
Mad at you, hungry, thirsty . . .

Is it not I
Who give our man
Water to wash his face
And to bathe?

Is it not I
Who nurse and soothe him
Like my own baby?

Does he not return to you
Clean shaven, smiling
Like a boy of fifteen?
Does he ever come home
With a dirty shirt?

But tell me, sister
Do you think
There is something wrong
With your husband
That he need
Have only one woman
For the rest of his life?
Do you feed him so well?

173

> Has the doctor told him
> That he has a heart disease
> And ordered him to sleep
> With only one woman
> For the rest of his life?[38]

Okot p'Bitek argues that the concubine is also a helping hand of the first wife, for she together with the man's first wife are engaged in bearing the load in him. Hence, the concubine has a definite contribution to that marriage and its well-being and should, for that reason, be treated with respect and justice.

It is much better if the wife faces these facts, however absurd they may be. Behind every man with a concubine, is a marriage with a miss somewhere. Sometimes it is from the concubine that the man gets the right perspective to begin to appreciate his wife. The problem is that the ship of marriage is entered into by many people when they have little or no knowledge of how much to expect from the married partner. It is a plunge where one explores the pool while in it. In the life of nearly every married man, particularly men who had had little knowledge of women before marriage, there comes a time when they feel that there are other better women outside the marriage who they must meet. This is, so often, the entry point of the concubine. Besides, many marriages live at the verge of divorce anyway.

Behind every marriage crisis, every divorce, there lies the history of a mediocre marriage, claims David Mace, in his book *Marriage: The art of lasting happiness*.[39] Sometimes that history goes back a long way. In some cases it goes back to the beginning. Divorce is the only final stage in a long process of deterioration. It is like death, which comes when disease has wasted the human frame to such feebleness that the spark of life can no longer survive.

The concubine comes to keep the flame of that marriage burning. Without the concubine, many marriages would not last. The man is perhaps waiting to make the right decision about his deteriorating marriage, but the concubine's presence tells him to hold on; perhaps the marriage would level itself up in the course of that waiting. Or he simply lets things drift on for the time being. It may be his own fault or the wife's that the marriage is sour; but in the meantime, the concubine will offer opportunity not only for a second thought but a longer dialogue and comparison.

In this context, the concubine has an important role to play in the society, general or even religious, in spite of her position being misunderstood and her presence cursed. For if the concubine is the nurse who treats the man's marital and psychological wounds, what makes her evil as she is said to be? Why is she not fully protected by the law?

Psychological problems of the concubine

A few of these have been mentioned above indirectly. But there is need to look into her mind more closely. Her position in the society, or rather her fate, throws her into:

(a) constant state of self-pity
(b) being suspicious of people
(c) the fear of death before she can make it in life
(d) the feeling of living in a state of sin or immorality
(e) the feeling that all persons other than those of her kind are against her; the law too.

She is in a constant state of self-pity because she fears that she might never make it in life. She wonders whether, for that matter, there is something wrong with her psychologically. She questions her own values. This is the awful feeling that, sometimes, has driven many to commit suicide or crimes. Hers is a sick spirit; she needs a psychiatrist to help her find her own feet and wings. She is suspicious of other people because she knows that she is not accepted or appreciated. Hardly anyone praises her for what she does. She is suspicious of other people because she knows that she is not accepted perhaps because she has been thrown into her present situation by the cruelty of other people. She fears being attacked by her rivals. Or perhaps by now she has been through many painful events that have taught her the virtue of not trusting anybody. The fear of death is more real to her against the wish and hope that one day she will make it in life and become somebody. At the back of her mind comes the terrifying whisper, 'I told you that you are a poor animal, now I will kill you!'

The feeling of being an immoral person is, perhaps, the most persistent one. By now, possibly, she has been called everything bad—tart, prostitute, devil, blood-sucker, stupid, bitch, and so on. It has been, as it were, that the public was out to brainwash her against herself. Experiencing some religious feelings, she tries to hide from her God because she thinks and feels that she has sinned too much to be before his eyes. She is not free at all to mix with the 'saved' and discuss God. This is the feeling that drives many concubines into great immorality and some into terrible drunkenness and crimes—all the time trying to kill that terrible bug in them which tells them that they are the wretched of the earth.

The feeling that her importance is counted only in the collection of population data for political purpose, does not make or encourage her to be a better citizen. She walks in the streets shamefully, wondering how many people are seeing and talking about her. She avoids public places where her enemies are likely to be. Therefore, she withdraws into the dark corners and paths. If anyone in the whole world welcomes her with a red carpet, that is the man who comes to her and makes all that warmth and exclusive experience for her.

How are her children, if she has any, treated by the public? How much sympathy should they expect from the public? Finally, what kind of citizens grow out of such children? These are important questions which are, as well, of national significance. The man who comes to see their lonely mother and talk to them too is, indeed, a very important person. He is a man of God in their own eyes. This is because in their conscious and unconscious prayers to their God, they are asking him to give them company, friendship, and love.

The man's helping hand

The problem with men who keep mistresses is the amount of lies they tell. The concubine is pinned down by a whole string of lies that include, perhaps, prospects for marriage when the divorce comes, or when the right time comes.

To be able to live up to one's lies is not easy. One lie deserves many other lies to cover it and yet it may never be covered completly. Eventually, the mistress discovers that this is not a man to be trusted. Given the circumstances of her background and her psychological pressures therefore, she decides that she can no longer afford to take him seriously and put all her eggs in his basket. She begins to see him as a passing cloud and, as the English proverb advises, she realises the importance of making hay while the sun shines. That is, now she will exploit him to the maximum while he lasts because she knows that tomorrow he is not going to come to her. What she should have liked to get from him tomorrow, she presses to have it today.

Back home, this man is furnishing his wife with a flood of lies. He mystifies his movements and adopts a non-commital language that excels. so much in African mentality. Or he becomes violent when she tries to probe his movements. The thing is, he wants his wife to trust him although he works against the foundation of that trust.

Would it not be good if he stopped lying and betraying his personality by facing the situation maturely? Many men who live a life of lies do not seem to be aware that, as the heads of their families, both what they say and what they do are being noticed and, perhaps, emulated by their children too. Hence, they are actually engaged in a course of demoralizing their family, for whatever affects the children's mother, affects the children too.

Such man could help the emotional stability of his women by displaying a personality worth trusting. There is nothing wrong in saying, 'Look here, I have a wife whom I do not intend to divorce. I love her and my children too, but I also love you for what you are to me.'

If the mistress develops a trust in him, she will certainly close the door to other men and keep him. Then he would not have to suffer from the feeling that she is simply using him and turning to other men as soon as he has gone out of her house. Of course, she is looking for a strong post to hold on to against her turbulent life, so why should she stick to a man who appears so unreliable?

It would be good to work out some kind of constitution with her. She should know the boundaries of his heart quite well. Only then would she be able to adjust to his satisfaction. He should know her problems and let her know his. After all, they come to each other because of something they miss without being with each other. They should form a sensible, honest team.

It does need a strong personality and emotional maturity though to admit that he has a mistress. It is not just the confession alone that is difficult, but he is worried by what follows after the confession. Many men are also afraid of what others would say. But the basic principle of life should be that what is good for one's existence and does not violate human respect and rights cannot, after all be bad.

Honesty is expensive, but it pays excellent dividends. It is more expensive emotionally and in practice too, to live dishonestly. In dishonesty, one sells one's personality at a throw-away price. It is so easy to tell lies, but it is so difficult to repair the damage done by those lies. A sensible person must respect himself and say only that which cannot cause embarrassment to him and to his family and friends in case of any echo. Many people who tell lies think or expect that the other person is not intelligent enough to see through the lie; or that if he discovers, the liar hopes, he will forget all about it soon. What the liar does not appear to know is that people are far more intelligent than they appear to the eye, and a lie is not easily forgotten once it has been discovered. A lie has too short legs, says a German proverb.

The African is a very complex person socially. You can keep on lying to a person who appears not to know that you are lying, and you would think that he is swallowing everything you tell him. For reasons that are culturally cultivated, he will never reveal to you by words that he is aware that you are lying, not until you have provoked him beyond his endurance which is quite substantial. So, he lets you live in a fool's world. This is because, basically, honesty is supposed to be lived but not merely spoken. Possibly all your African relatives, friends, and colleagues keep the register of your lies which you have told them even though they present to you an innocent face. If you have been lying and you are clever, you will discover that something somewhere is amiss because they do not appear to trust you or take you seriously any more. But by then, your relationship with them is irreparably damaged.

The wife and the concubine

The biggest challenge to a man who has a mistress is whether or not to tell his wife or family of the existence of that other woman. If he tells her, he knows what to expect, yet he knows the amount of risk he is taking by keeping silent about it until his wife discovers it. The majority of such men keep silent about the affair hoping that they will find a way to contain the reaction of the wife when the truth comes to her. Until then, he will have to live by substantial lying so that when he is going north to meet this woman, he says he is going south. Then follows the classic lies when he comes home late:

—I was working overtime
—I went to see a colleague of mine
—I was at the bar
—I went on a short trip
—My stomach is upset, I can't eat tonight.
—My car broke down

When his wife questions him further suspiciously, he picks up a quarrel or a fight with her, or begins to find faults with her.

—You women are short-sighted
—You are ungrateful
—How can I be late to come to my own home?
—You have nothing to discuss with me peacefully when I come home
—You are a terrible nagger
—You do not know how to talk

Let us say that Musa has an affair that does not seem to die out. One day he comes home and tells his wife, 'I am sorry, there is something happening . . . There is this woman—Dorothy . . .'

For sure, there will be a big fight in that home when the Dorothy surfaces. However, what follows after that is not as bad as if Musa's wife had discovered that Dorothy herself. After the discovery, her trust for the husband would be ruined. The discovery bruises her so much that in the future whatever he says, truth or untruth, she will be forced to suspect. Whereas if he had revealed that Dorothy himself, his wife would still retain a sense of trust in him. She will reflect on the confession that, if her husband could be that honest as to reveal his lover to her, he should be basically an honest man; therefore, he is likely to tell her when things go wrong from his side. As the result, she should relax and trust him even more.

Such is a healthy feeling. The confessed Dorothy is easier to forgive than the discovered one.

The right and wrong of keeping a concubine

Saying that it is wrong to have a concubine already establishes a definite stand. Same as saying that it is right to keep one. Where does one stand while making that statement?

Most people who claim that keeping a concubine is wrong, approach it from the religous point of view, usually from a Christian stance. But as to whether their feeling is right in the eyes of God, that is another matter. There is nothing the pastor seems to dread more than being confronted with the question, 'Do you think there is a situation in life that justifies sexual intercourse with a woman who is not one's wife?'

For hypothetical purposes, let us say that having a concubine is wrong. That statement poses the questions: Why is it wrong? To whom is it wrong? Does that overlook the fact that there may be other reasons, accidental, economic, pathological or cultural that could lead a man to concubinage?

We are not trying to justify some kind of free-love as it is usually called. What should be noted however is that Nature or God does not let man build too tall towers, or as a German proverb puts it, trees do not grow to touch the sky. When man builds such towers while he does not and is supposed not to live in a perfect world, Nature has a way of breaking them.

The question of what is sin and what is not cannot even be answered easily from a religious point of view. A widow may want to know from her God who her husband is or who will attend to her emotional needs after God has taken away her husband through death. Is it more Christian to have organized prostitution, marital infidelity with impunity, a rapid growing divorce rate and increasing number of illegitimate children, than polygamy?, asks Ralph Dodge in his book *The Unpopular Missionary*.[40] Is it more Christian for young women to become prostitutes, call-girls or mistresses, than to become second or third wives of respected family members? These are some of the founding questions. But let us modify Dodge's questions in and through concubinage: Is it more religious and more in keeping with civilization to ignore the problems of the single woman? When the scriptures say that we should help one another, be generous to one another, be kind to one another, do they draw boundaries between physical and spiritual needs? When the single girl cannot find a man to marry not even as a fourth wife, does it mean that her God has, therefore, condemned her emotional requirements and that no man should dare touch her?

However philosophically or religiously we may like to respond to these questions, the founding truth is that, first and foremost, they refer to the human being. In religion we learn that it is God who creates people, not Satan. Consequently, one can conclude accurately that God creates a blind man because he knows that he has created other people with eyes and who should help the blind, otherwise he himself would be a blind God.

It is said that what God has not provided, man should provide. As another saying goes that God made man and man made the city. The wretched of the earth are the respnsibility of the fortunate of the earth. God creates people and things in their diversities so that they may become dependant upon each other as an appreciation of a common thought of creation.

When a pastor is confronted with a situation of a girl who has conceived and given birth out of wedlock, he does not know exactly what to say about it. It appears to have been preached indirectly that those who are married are better people in the eyes of God than those who are not married; and that children born to married parents are more of God's children than those born out of wedlock.

Correct?

What about the belief that all people are a creation of God? Is it true to say that, the creator, God, has as much love while creating the so-called bastard as he has while creating that son of the Most-Reverend Profesor Peep? Whom does God love more than the other— the concubine called Anowa or the wife of Pastor Mwaka?

It is also in this discussion that the story of the prostitute brought to Christ comes in focus. They brought her to him, hoping that Christ would give them the greenlight to stone her to death because she had been caught in the very act. Instead, Christ is said to have addressed her as 'Sister.' He asked anyone among them who had brought her to cast the first stone if he knew that he himself was sinless. None of them picked up a stone and hit her with it. They all went away, one by one. And Christ forgave and sent her away. That made him more of a God than a human being.

I think we become better human beings only when we bear fully the responsibility of human problems sympathetically as a creation of one God. But the problem with the human being is his ambition and desire to judge others, yet the scriptures instruct, 'Don't judge lest you be judged. Before you remove the flake in the other person's eye, remove the log in your eye.' In the kingdom of God, wherever and whenever it might be, surely, there shall be many people who were so-called evil-doers on earth. If the right theology is that God cannot give his child a stone when that child asks for bread, why should anyone think that God should not be kind, loving, understanding and forgiving even to those we consider evil because they do what we do not authorize?

Given the chance to choose between two evils, it is better to choose the lesser evil. If concubinage is a less evil than prostituion, it is better to go for it. We begin to learn and develop for the better by accepting the necessary evil as the starting point to development towards excellence. The suffering of the helpless among the capable and fortunate should be punished on the fortunate. As the saying goes, he who eats with a blindman must feed him. There is no sensible religion or ethics that should overlook the fact that dependence is a factor and component of every situation of life. How can we say that blessed are the merciful when we limit that mercy? How can we love one another when we limit the dimensions of that love?

NOTES:

1. Alvin Toffler, *Future Shock* (Pan Books, London, 1970). p. 267.
2. Schillebeeck, Marriage: Secular Reality and Saving Mystery, 1, p. 284.
3. Eugene, Hillman, *Polygamy Reconsidered*, (Orbis Books, New York, 1975), p. 140-145.
4. Jerome Carcopino, *Daily Life in the Ancient Rome* (Yale University Press, New Haven, 1940): Hardmondsworth: Penguin Books, 1964), p. 94.
5. Michael Lawson, *Roman Law: A Source of Canonical Marriage Lesgislation,* Resonance 3, (Spring, 1967), p.9.
6. See Lawson, *Roman Law,* p.9-14.
7. L.W.Banard, *Justin Martyr: His Life and Thought* (Cambridge University Press, London and New York, 1967), p. 46.
8. See Hillman, *Polygamy Reconsidered*, p. 20.
9. Saint Augustine, *De bono conjugali,* quoted by Hillman in *Polygamy Reconsidered*, p. 21..
10. See No. 9. p. 21.
11. See No. 9. p. 21.
12. Will Burnham, *Chronology of Church History,* (Evangel Publishing House, 1975) p. 27.
13. Napoleon Hill, *Think and Grow Rich* (A Fawcet Crest Book, New York, 1960) p. 176-177.
14. See Hill, *Think and Grow Rich,* p. 177.
15. See Hill, *Think and Grow Rich,* p. 117.
16. John Mbiti, *African Religions and Philosophy* (Heinemann Educational Books London, 1970), p. 142.
17. Claude Levi-Strauss, *The Scope of Anthropolgy* (Jonathan Cape, London, 1967), p. 47.
18. J.C. Carothers, *The Mind of Man in Africa* (Tom Stacey, London, 1972), p. 110.
119. Julius Nyerere, *Ujamaa,* (Oxford University Press, London, 1968), p. 6-7.
20. See Mbiti, *African Religions and Philosophy,* p. 144.
21. David R. Mace, *Marriage: The Art of Lasting happiness* (Hodder and Stroughton, London, 1964), p. 108.

22. Dale Carnegie, *How to Win Friends and Influence People*, (The World's Work, Kingswood, Surrey, 1964).
23. D.F. Horrobin, *Science is God*, (Medical and Technical Publishing Co. Ltd., London, 1969), p. 102.
24. See Horrobin, *Science is God*, p. 102.
25. See Mbiti, *African Religions and Philosophy*, p. 48.
26. Placide Tempels, *Bantu Philosophy* (Presence Africaine, France, 1969), p. 135.
27. See Hillman, *Polygamy Reconsidered*, p. 64.
28. Wambui wa Karanja, (Paper: *Outside Wives and Inside Wives in Nigeria: A Study of Changing Perceptions in Marriage*), p. 9.
29. See No. 29, p. 10-11.
30. See No. 29, p. 20.
31. See No. 29, p. 20.
32. See No. 29, p. 18-19.
33. See Hillman, *Polygamy Reconsidered*, p. 109.
34. See No. 29, p. 18-19.
35. Charles Otieno, *My Second Mother*, article published in 'Men Only' (Trend Publication, Nairobi, 1984) Vol. 1, No. 4.
36. See No. 29, p. 18-19.
37. Charles Cinda, *Loved in Tandem*, (Men Only) see No. 35, p. 29.
38. Okot p'Bitek, *Two Songs* (East African Publishing House, Nairobi, 1971), p. 148-152.
39. See Mace, *Marriage: The art of lasting happiness*, p. 118.
40. *Ralph Dodge, The Unpopular Missionary* (Westwood, N.J., 1964), p. 145.

SELECTED BIBLIOGRAPHY

1. Hillman Eugene, *Polygamy Reconsidered*, Orbis Books, Maryknoll, N. Y., 1974.
2. Hastings Adrian, *Christian Marriage in Africa*, S.P.C.K., London, 1974
3. Mbiti John S, *African Religions and Philosophy*, Heinemann Educational Books, London, 1970.
4. Shorter Aylward W.F., *African Culture and the Christian Church*, Geoggrey Chapman, London, 1974.
5. Philips Arthur & Morris Henry F, *Marriage Laws in Africa*, Oxford University Press, London, 1971.
6. Allmen von J.J., *Marriage*, Oxford University Press, N. Y., 1958.
7. Schapera!., *Married Life in an African Tribe*, Faber & Faber Ltd., London.
8. Diop cheikh Anta, *The African Origin of Civilization:* Myth or Reality, Lawrence Hill & Company, N. Y., 1974.
9. Hammond-Tooke W.D., *The Bantu Speaking Peoples of Southern Africa*, Routledge & Kegan Paul, London and Boston, 1974.
10. Nyerere Julius, *Ujamaa*, University Press, London, 1968.
11. Carothers. JK.C., *The Mind of Man in Africa*, Tom Stacey, Londopn, 1972.
12. Mace David, Marriage: *The art of lasting happiness*, Hodder & Stoughton, London, 1964.
13. P'Bitek Okot, *Two Songs*, East African Publishing House, Nairobi, 1971.
14. Onwuejeogwu Angulu M., *The Social Anthropology of Africa*, Heinemann Educational Books, Ibadan, 1975.

INDEX